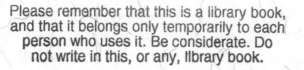

THE
EXTERNAL
DEGREE

Cyril O. Houle

Foreword by Samuel B. Gould
Epilogue by John Summerskill

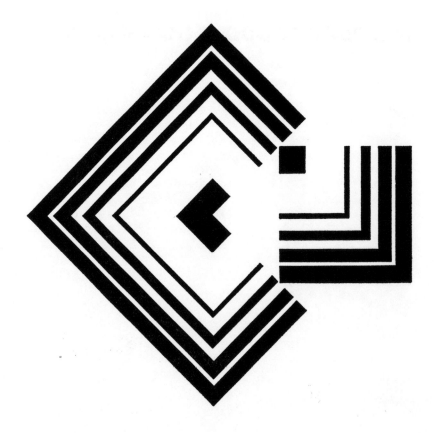

THE EXTERNAL DEGREE

Jossey-Bass Publishers
San Francisco · Washington · London · 1974

THE EXTERNAL DEGREE
by Cyril O. Houle

Copyright © 1973 by: Jossey-Bass, Inc., Publishers
615 Montgomery Street
San Francisco, California 94111
and
Jossey-Bass Limited
3 Henrietta Street
London WC2E 8LU

Library of Congress Catalogue Card Number LC 73-3775

International Standard Book Number ISBN 0-87589-175-6

Manufactured in the United States of America

JACKET DESIGN BY WILLI BAUM

FIRST EDITION
    First printing: June 1973
    Second printing: February 1974

Code 7318

The
Jossey-Bass Series
in Higher Education

A publication of the
Commission on Non-Traditional Study

Foreword

$\mathcal{T}$*he External Degree* is a vital part of the report of the Commission on Non-Traditional Study, *Diversity by Design* (Jossey-Bass, 1973), even though it appears independently. The Commission (whose members are listed elsewhere) was an independent group established cooperatively by the College Entrance Examination Board and the Educational Testing Service and financed chiefly by those two organizations and the Carnegie Corporation. The mandate of the Commission was to look broadly at all forms of undergraduate non-traditional education and to make recommendations concerning it. While *The External Degree* is complete in itself, some minor duplication exists in contents between it and *Diversity by Design.* This slight overlapping was necessary to preserve the independence of each volume and avoid the inconvenience to the reader caused by cross-referencing.

From the beginning of the deliberations of the Commission, it was clear to us that the current movement toward the use of the external degree is by itself a large and significant subject. We realized that if we were to include in the Commission's one-volume report all that should be said, the external degree would overshadow all other aspects of non-traditional study. Thus we decided to deal with it in a separate statement.

The question of authorship was an easy one to settle. Cyril O. Houle is an outstanding authority on adult and continuing education. He has devoted his life to the field as teacher, scholar, practitioner, author, and lecturer, both in the United States and abroad. Thus his credentials for such a book are impeccable. In addition he was a member of the Commission and was very actively involved in the preparation of *Diversity by Design*.

John Summerskill was a logical choice to sum up what is happening at the present time. As director of the Office of External Degree Programs (later called the Office of New Degree Programs) of the College Entrance Examination Board and the Educational Testing Service, he had the opportunity to travel widely, to see perceptively, and to react to what he saw. His Epilogue is a vital addition to our knowledge and interpretation of current events.

The backgrounds of the two men are interesting to consider in relation to the assignment given them. Mr. Summerskill was at one time a vice-president at Cornell, the great archetype of the utilitarian university, and later president of San Francisco State University, an important prototype of the modern urban university. Mr. Houle, as a dean of extension activities at The University of Chicago, pioneered in offering adults both degree and certificate programs which were progenitors of many later developments. He has also had as graduate students a number of people who went on to create programs of special degrees for adults at other colleges and universities. They are men and women of thought, but particularly of thought leading to action.

Mr. Houle presents here a definitive and scholarly piece of work, possibly the most comprehensive to date. He sets the stage with a historical statement that places the present surge of interest in the external degree (in other countries as well as in the United States) into appropriate perspective. He then makes a careful analysis of the potential and actual clientele for more education and the factors that have brought the external degree to the foreground as a major way of filling a widespread need. He goes on to describe some visible and significant experiments in establishing such a degree. Finally, he identifies and discusses the issues that confront the designers, administrators, supporters, and users of external degree programs.

With matters as they are in higher education, some people always cry out loudly that it is one minute to midnight. Others are equally insistent that time is of no consequence, that the higher learning is ageless. Both are wrong in Mr. Houle's view. He moves between the two extreme attitudes calmly and judiciously, refuting myths with data and countering prejudices with facts. For example, in dealing with the often-expressed fear that expansion of educational opportunity will lead to a lowering of the average ability of students in higher education, he presents studies conducted in Great Britain and the United States showing that such fears have no basis in fact. He quotes (in Chapter Three) Paul Taubman and Terence Wales, who, after analyzing the changes from the mid-1920s to the mid-1960s, said, "It is apparent that the quality of college students has not declined. In fact, throughout this period of forty years, during which a substantially greater percentage of high school graduates entered college, it has even noticeably increased." This is a mighty argument for offering the external degree to those adults who demonstrated their ability in high school but ended their formal education at that point or who did not complete college work.

Similarly Mr. Houle's treatment of the issues surrounding external degrees reflects the Commission's unanimous concern for high standards in every aspect of higher education. More rather than less rigor is demanded of the external degree student; more rather than less initiative is expected. A high degree of motivation is a fundamental requisite. The most careful monitoring of innovative adaptations and departures from the norm is necessary, not to discourage flexible and diverse approaches but to make certain that each person has a truly educative experience. An institution that chooses a non-traditional direction opens itself to extraordinary scrutiny and must ultimately be able to prove the worth of the way it has chosen.

It is too early to tell how many institutions will succeed in offering non-traditional study. But the possibilities are available as well as the tools. The temperate tone of *The External Degree,* its avoidance of strict prescriptions of what to do and how, its identification of exciting beginnings together with its awareness of dangerous slippage, and above all its deep faith in the broadening educational needs of a democratic society make it a significant document about an unusually significant movement.

March 1973   SAMUEL B. GOULD
                            Chairman
                            Commission on Non-Traditional Study

Preface

Edgar Allen Poe once observed that "in one case out of a hundred a point is excessively discussed because it is obscure; in the ninety-nine remaining it is obscure because excessively discussed."[1] Wherever cause and effect may properly lie in the present case, virtually everyone would agree that the external degree is obscure, and many would say that it has been excessively discussed.

The term itself has come to have countless meanings, some explicitly stated and others detectable only by inference. A few people would argue that the University of London has a patent on the term, while others would staunchly assert that London has not awarded a separate external degree since it started conferring internal degrees in the early part of the twentieth century. Some proponents accept other institutions as having worked out the only "right" pattern—among them, the British Open University, Empire State College, the New York State Board of Regents, the Extended University of the University of California, the University Without Walls.

Still other analysts of the external degree center their atten-

---

[1] "The Rationale of Verse," *Southern Literary Messenger,* October 1848, *14,* 577.

tion not upon institutional patterns but upon ways of work, a few of which can be suggested here. Some stress a form of teaching, such as the use of television, videotapes, contracts, or mentors. Some argue for a method of learning, such as individualized study, unsupervised experience, or the completion of programs not sponsored by colleges and universities but by the armed services, proprietary schools, business, industry, or other organizations which offer instruction. Some advance the claims of special kinds of evaluation, such as specific or general examinations, the assembly of portfolios, or the judgments of committees of assessment. And some argue for the summation into a coherent whole of learning experiences and credentials which have been acquired in many ways.

Partly because people are at cross-purposes in considering the degree, their discussion of it is often emotional, ranging from euphoric acceptance to bitter rejection. Those who believe that their long-held dreams are now being widely accepted or who catch glimpses of a previously undreamed-of future of educational opportunity for everyone are likely to accept whatever they hear uncritically and to be ready to abandon past standards of accomplishment or to set new ones which have never been critically validated. Those who feel that their own programs are threatened or that the new degree has a dubious or incapable sponsorship are likely to reject any change regardless of its merits. But few people are at or near the extremes of the continuum. Most policy makers and educators in institutions of higher learning have been aware for some years that the patterns of the past could not continue into the future unchanged. And many people in both groups have turned with open minds and an inquiring spirit to examine the external degree as at least one solution to the problems which beset them.

The purpose of *The External Degree* is to help them in this assessment. Its theme is that the external degree is not a simple but a complex phenomenon; it includes all the special approaches already mentioned and others as well. It has been produced by long-developing changes in American society and in its colleges and universities. The external degree, both in the United States and abroad, has developed in several generalized and many specific forms. Some have been successful and some have failed, but most are so new that their sponsors are still in the process of discovering whether these patterns can thrive in modern society. While problems are clear and often stark, both for individual institutions and for the whole society, the solutions (or, in some cases, the processes by which solutions will ultimately be found) are becoming clear as alternative pathways to progress are charted. *The External Degree,* then, is an exploration of a social and educational movement—its past, its temporary present, and the hopes of its leaders for the future.

In writing the following pages, I have benefitted from the help of many people. Three meetings sponsored by the Commission on Non-Traditional Study contributed greatly to the shaping of *The External Degree.* One was a session of the full Commission devoted largely to reports and discussions of the external degree. The second was a conference held under Educational Testing Service (ETS) auspices and guided by Harold J. Alford of its staff; at this meeting, directors of degree programs from all over the United States were brought together to describe their work and to discuss issues. Third, a small subcommittee of the Commission (made up up Charles A. LeMaistre, Stephen H. Spurr, Samuel B. Gould, John Summerskill, and myself) spent a day discussing the topic intensively.

As the Commission proceeded with its work, it felt the need of additional data, and therefore additional funding was secured by ETS from the Carnegie Corporation and the Educational Foundation of America. These funds supported a data-gathering effort directed by K. Patricia Cross and John R. Valley and expedited by Wesley W. Walton. These studies will eventually result in a series of research monographs, but some of the findings are incorporated both in *The External Degree* and in *Diversity by Design.* The results of three studies are particularly relevant to the present discussion and are acknowledged at various places throughout the book.

The first study, of the *demand* for non-traditional education, was carried out and will be reported by Richard E. Peterson and Abraham Carp of ETS on the basis of data collected by the Response Analysis Corporation. This study reports the results of a national sample of actual students and would-be students between the ages of eighteen and sixty not attending college full-time.

The second study, on the *supply* of non-traditional education, was carried out by the Center for Research and Development in Higher Education at the University of California, Berkeley, and will be reported by Janet Ruyle, JB Lon Hefferlin, Lucy Ann Geiselman, and Ann Kirton. It reports the results of a survey of non-traditional practices now being conducted at all institutions of higher learning in the United States. Several special tabulations concerning the external degree were made for this volume by Ruyle.

The third study was also carried out by the Center for Research and Development in Higher Education at the University of California, Berkeley. It involved twenty-five interviews conducted and summarized by Mel Bloom, Ruyle, and Hefferlin with *leaders* of non-traditional programs and institutions. Since the interviews were confidential, the anonymity of the persons concerned is preserved in this book and, in a few cases, minor details are changed for that purpose.

Many other people helped me, either directly or by correspondence, to secure the data and achieve the understanding necessary for writing *The External Degree*. It would be impossible to name them all but certain key figures at the College Entrance Examination Board (CEEB) and ETS can not go unmentioned. They are Jack N. Arbolino, George H. Hanford, Robert J. Solomon, John Summerskill, John A. Valentine, and John R. Valley. I particularly regret that Mr. Summerskill could not continue with our original plans of joint authorship. The next-to-final draft of the manuscript received the benefit of a close reading by the following people who were good enough to give me detailed suggestions for change: Florence Anderson, Samuel B. Gould, JB Lon Hefferlin, Fred A. Nelson, and John Valley. Jane D. Wirsig, of ETS gave editorial guidance and skillful direction at every stage in the preparation of the manuscript and solved many problems along the way. My debt to Samuel B. Gould, particularly for helping me understand the broad academic strategies and inner workings of institutions of higher learning, is so great that I do not have words to express it.

As the Bibliographic Essay shows, the topic of the external degree ramifies in many directions. Betsy Walkup and William A. Mahler were of great assistance in uncovering and analyzing source materials, and Peter Cookson, Peter Hayward, and Neil Wilkof also provided valuable assistance. Various secretaries at ETS and at the Commission offices typed early versions of the document; and Shirley Johnson, Florence Kiey, and Camille Nini were valuable in facilitating production of the manuscript. Dolores Ford, as always, did an incomparably skillful job of preparing the final draft.

The external degree is so broad and protean a phenomenon that one cannot be satisfied that he has dealt with it adequately. Furthermore, he can be certain that at least the details of what he says will soon be out-of-date, perhaps even before his words reach print. Let me make it clear therefore that despite all the help given me by others, I had absolute freedom to state my own understandings and viewpoints and am completely accountable for any errors or misjudgments which the reader may find. If they are not evident on the day of publication, they soon will be. Otherwise the major thesis of this book—that the external degree is now in a period of dynamic growth—will have been proved false.

Chicago   CYRIL O. HOULE
March 1973

Contents

Commission on
Non-Traditional Study

SAMUEL B. GOULD—*chairman; chancellor emeritus,
State University of New York*

M. ROBERT ALLEN—*dean, Division of Continuing
Education, University of Miami*

HOWARD R. BOWEN—*chancellor, Claremont
University Center*

MARY I. BUNTING—*assistant to the president for
special projects, Princeton University*

HENRY CHAUNCEY—*president, Interuniversity
Communications Council, Inc.* (EDUCOM)

ARLAND F. CHRIST-JANER*—*president,
College Entrance Examination Board*

FRED C. COLE—*president, Council on Library Resources*

JOSEPH P. COSAND—*professor of education,
Center for Higher Education,
University of Michigan*

BERTRAM H. DAVIS—*general secretary, American
Association of University Professors*

WALTER G. DAVIS—*director, Department of Education,
American Federation of Labor and Congress
of Industrial Organizations*

FRANK G. DICKEY—*executive director, National
Commission on Accrediting*

W. TODD FURNISS—*director, Commission on Academic
Affairs, American Council on Education*

RICHARD C. GILMAN—*president, Occidental College*

CYRIL O. HOULE—*professor of education,
University of Chicago*

C. ALBERT KOOB—*president, National Catholic
Educational Association*

ELIZABETH D. KOONTZ—*director, Women's Bureau,
U. S. Department of Labor*

CHARLES A. LEMAISTRE—*chancellor, The University
of Texas System*

JOHN W. MACY, JR.—*former president, Corporation
for Public Broadcasting*

LELAND L. MEDSKER—*Center for Research and
Development in Higher Education,
University of California*

JAMES PARTON—*chairman of the executive committee,
Encyclopaedia Britannica Educational Corporation*

JAMES A. PERKINS—*chairman of the board and
chief executive officer, International Council for
Educational Development*

ALICE RIVLIN—*senior fellow, Brookings Institution*

FELIX C. ROBB—*director, Southern Association
of Colleges and Schools*

STEPHEN H. SPURR—*president, University of Texas
at Austin*

WILLIAM W. TURNBULL*—*president, Educational
Testing Service*

CLIFTON R. WHARTON, JR.—*president, Michigan
State University*

JOHN A. VALENTINE—*executive secretary*

FLORENCE G. KIEY—*executive assistant*

   * *Ex officio members of the Commission*

THE
EXTERNAL
DEGREE

Emergence of the American External Degree

ᚼᚼᚼᚼᚼᚼᚼᚼᚼᚼᚼᚼᚼᚼᚼᚼᚼᚼᚼᚼᚼᚼᚼᚼᚼᚼᚼ

The treatises that are written on university reform may be acute or not, but their chief value to the observer is the showing that a cleavage is occurring in the hitherto firm granite of the past, and a new era is nearly arrived.

RALPH WALDO EMERSON

*L*ate in 1970, the external degree came suddenly and powerfully to the attention of the American academic community. Strong voices spoke out in its behalf; several universities and university systems made plans to initiate it, others announced serious studies; new colleges to provide it were created; foundations made substantial grants; and magazines and newspapers began to describe, analyze, support, and condemn it.

The Open University, when announced in Great Britain, immediately became an object of intense curiosity and occasionally of undiscriminating support, though reports reaching America as to its nature were varied. On the whole, the president of the Carnegie Corporation appeared to be correct (and provided perhaps as good a brief definition as can be devised) when he said that "the external degree—one that can be earned by a student outside of the normal institutional framework—is an idea whose time seems to have come in this country."[1]

Uncritical acceptance of the new degree by some was at once countered by skepticism by others. Experienced veterans of the world of higher education are well aware of its fascination with new ideas and devices put forward as panaceas for all current ills. The executive vice-president of the College Entrance Examination Board said in an address on the subject: "Candor moves me to begin by confessing that I had a very difficult time deciding whether to talk with you about hula hoops or miniature golf. In my lifetime both have been fads which took the country by storm—in much the same way that the external degree promises to become the current 'thing' in higher education."[2] He went on to say that, after all the excited talk had subsided, he believed a few solid and enduring programs would remain.

The talk has now somewhat subsided, and solid programs are being shaped and put into effect. Meanwhile increased understanding of the external degree is emerging; it is a worldwide phenomenon with deep roots and antecedents traceable to 1534. It appears to offer at least one solution for such major problems of American higher education as inadequate financing, the high dropout rate, and the undereducation of women. The teaching technology and evaluative processes required to sustain at least some forms of service are already well advanced. Meanwhile the number of proposals for new programs is continuing to grow steadily even as the concept of the external degree is causing many old programs to be seen in a new light.

[1] A. Pifer, "Is It Time for an External Degree?" *College Board Review,* Winter 1970–1971, *78,* 5.

[2] G. H. Hanford, "The Open University, the External Degree, and Continuing Education," unpublished address at a conference of the Directors' Roundtable for Adult and Continuing Education, April 29, 1971.

This book assesses the external degree: by describing its historical roots and some of its best-established examples here and abroad; identifying reasons why it will probably be a more prominent aspect of academic life in the future than it has been in the past; exploring the major ideas and themes around which the new proposals are centered; and considering the issues which arise as the external degree is absorbed into the practices of American colleges and universities. Since the baccalaureate receives major attention in most discussions of the degree, it occupies center stage here; but the associate in arts, the master's degree, and the doctorate are also considered at various points as seems appropriate.

Internal-Degree Patterns

The external degree can best be understood by placing it in historical perspective. In the United States, two essentially different patterns of basic requirements for the academic degree have existed. Both of them, however, have until recently led only to internal degrees. The first, which began with the founding of Harvard College in 1636 and lasted for a quarter of a millennium, defined the degree as an award for completing a set course of studies pursued by all students in the same fashion and in the same sequence; few alternatives were given the individual, though he might enrich his program by adding optional activities and making use of literary societies, which were central to the cultural life of the college. In the beginning, the content of the curriculum was classical and the ethos puritanically religious, but during the eighteenth and nineteenth centuries a gradual broadening of scope occurred. Examples of such wholly prescribed pattern are still found, and such a pattern is occasionally advanced in whole or in part as an experimental venture—the curriculum of St. John's College and the Chicago College plan of the 1930s and 1940s are examples.

The second pattern of degree requirements, rooted in efforts to democratize higher education, was initiated most dramatically when Charles W. Eliot established the elective system at Harvard in a series of hard-fought academic battles in the last thirty years of the nineteenth century. The idea of freedom of choice among courses was scarcely a novel one in this country; Thomas Jefferson, for example, intended that it characterize the work of the University of Virginia, but Eliot finally put the new principle dramatically into effect. The decision to allow the student some range of choice was recognized as having profound consequences, both immediate and far-reaching. Albert Jay Nock suggested sixty years later while discussing the elective system that "the worst calamity that ever befell American education was Eliot's refusal of the presidency of a textile manufacturing company."[3]

The impact of the elective system led almost immediately to other innovations. The United States did not separate instruction from evaluation by adopting the European pattern of comprehensive examinations. Instead it divided content into refined and specialized units and overlaid various patterns on these basic units. Colleges and universities developed the concepts of course credit, concentration and distribution of content, majors and minors based on firmly structured departments, a minimum number of credits for graduation, grade points, differentials in academic accounting between classroom and laboratory hours of instruction and between lower and upper division courses, and other rules and processes now so familiar that they almost seem to have been in existence forever.

The net effect of these changes was that the baccalaureate degree began to be awarded on the basis of the accumulation of a suitable number and variety of hours of credit at an average level of accomplishment. Even advanced degrees, based in part on the passing of comprehensive examinations and the writing of theses, required a number of credit courses. This system allows for almost endless adaptation to various institutional forms and bodies of content. The practical college or university, such as Cornell and the public land-grant colleges, could flourish under this system as could the research university based on the German model; both these new forms were well established by the end of the nineteenth century. The openness of the system led to a proliferation in the degrees awarded in American higher education. In 1877 there were 11; ten years later, there were 60; a decade after that, 242; by 1960, there were more than 1600.[4]

[3] A. J. Nock, *A Journal of These Days* (New York: Morrow, 1934).
[4] W. C. Eells, *Degrees in Higher Education* (Washington, D.C.: Center for Applied Research in Education, 1963), pp. 1–7.

This diversification has led to the observation—usually the complaint—that an American degree no longer has any consistent and coherent meaning. In 1908 Eliot observed, with evident pride, that none of the Harvard degrees at any level had "any definite signification in regard to subjects of study or specific achievements."[5] A British royal commission quoted him with approval in 1913, pointing out that the same situation prevailed in its country, and went on to remark in a passage which, as later pages of this book will show, is relevant to current American discussions, "we therefore think that any attempt to equate internal and external degrees with each other is hopeless. We may add that we think it unnecessary."[6]

But an underlying assumption of both the prescribed and the elective American degree patterns, so profound that it has seldom been stated, was that they were to be secured only by full-time study by young people (mostly men) in residence on the campus of a college or university. Both patterns were, in a word, internal. The first was so rigid that it could allow only study of this sort. The student must march along in step with his contemporaries through the same curriculum. If he dropped out, he might later return, but on a full-time basis. And, since each college had its own program, transfer between institutions was almost impossible.

The assumption that study should be wholly internal was gradually undermined by the elective system, its flexibility allowing able and energetic individuals who could not concentrate full-time on study to accumulate course credits on a part-time basis and eventually to secure a degree. Moreover, the fact that virtually all institutions of higher learning came to use the same general academic accounting systems and degree criteria meant that one could accumulate credit by study at several different campuses, though the

[5] C. W. Eliot, *University Administration* (Boston: Houghton Mifflin, 1908), p. 167. Here, as elsewhere, Eliot gives a closely reasoned argument for his case, but it can perhaps be summed up in the statement that "it is one of the great advantages of the elective system that the intelligent, self-directing, responsible student can have all the advantages of freedom, while the irresponsible, thoughtless, or lazy student can be made to do some work, without driving him into studies for which he has no capacity and in which he feels no interest."

[6] Royal Commission on University Education in London, *Final Report* (London: His Majesty's Stationery Office, 1913), p. 12.

student usually lost some ground when he transferred to another college or university, and his final cluster of courses almost always had to be taken at the degree-granting institution.

Thus the number of part-time students grew. The degrees they secured were still internal degrees; it simply took longer to win them. The two prevailing American views about such students were suggested in 1967 to an English audience by the president of the Council of Graduate Schools in the United States:

> *The part-time graduate student . . . has been more sinned against than sinning. And the sins that have been committed against him came, as usual, from the best humanitarian motives. Here is a poor fellow, struggling against great odds to get an education and a degree that he needs. Let's help him all we can. He doesn't quite meet admission requirements to the university. Well, perhaps motivation will compensate for lack of achievement. Let's give him a chance. That's the first sin, and it leads to all the rest of them. He's not doing very well in his classes, he is frequently absent, he doesn't participate actively in seminar. The poor man is probably tired after a hard day's work; his wife probably nags him. But he's obviously trying, so let's give him the benefit of the doubt and pass him along. And so it goes the second year and perhaps the third, and at the end he may disappear or he may even pass his examinations. But whether he does or not, it has not been a satisfying experience for him and certainly not for his teachers.*
>
> *Perhaps this doesn't happen here, but I can assure you it happens in the United States. At least it did happen until we finally discovered a simple fact: the fewer adjustments you make for the part-time student, the better for him and for all concerned. To begin with, he should meet the same high standards for admission to graduate school that all others have to meet. His performance in graduate school should be maintained at the same level as that of others, and finally, and perhaps most importantly, he should move along toward his degree objective at a pace as near as possible to that which we call "normal progress." It may be*

that your universities can permit a more leisurely pace. We cannot do it.[7]

Extension Degree

As the number of part-time students, both undergraduate and graduate, grew in the early years of the twentieth century, the task of fitting them into internal-degree sequences became ever more difficult. The university extension movement offered one solution to this problem. The idea that universities should take education to the general adult public had been imported from England in the 1880s, had experienced a mushroom growth, and then had died away. But soon after the turn of the century, the idea was taken up again, particularly by the general state universities, the urban universities, and the land-grant colleges; the provision of credit courses seemed a natural way to meet the needs of adults. Various facilitative arrangements helped take instruction to these students: creating convenient instructional centers, often off campus; offering late afternoon, evening, or weekend courses; using correspondence and, later on, radio and television instruction; and concentrating courses into short periods of time, particularly during the summer.

At first these efforts were simply ways of facilitating the acquisition of internal degrees, but a logical next step occurred when some universities decided to offer an entire degree program by extension. No two universities have worked out the same way of doing this, and patterns of control and administration are constantly changing. In the late 1950s, James T. Carey studied the adult education divisions of 194 universities. He found that 32 percent of these divisions had programs dominated by the established departments of instruction, only a part-time evening director, and little or no budget. Twenty-nine percent had reached a stage of autonomous development with a full-time coordinator and a budget of up to half a million dollars. Twenty-six percent had a dean and a staff with a budget of up to a million dollars. In 13 percent a full-scale college had emerged with a staff of administrators, at least a small full-time

[7] G. O. Arlt, "Of Time and the Pierian Spring," in *The University Education of Mature Students* (London: Birkbeck College, University of London, 1967), p. 23.

faculty, a budget of over a million dollars, and a well-established separate identity within the university.[8] These adult educational units, called by many different names, are usually described generically as extension divisions or evening colleges.

Despite the degree of independence achieved, most of the requirements for extension degrees sponsored by adult education divisions strongly resemble those for the internal degrees offered by the same universities. The twenty-eight-year-old man or woman is treated in almost the same way as the eighteen-year old. A successful author must study freshman composition, a manager is required to take elementary accounting, and a bilingual student is told that he must enroll in six courses to meet the foreign language requirement. If the internal student is expected to pass forty courses, each meeting three hours a week for a semester, so is the external student. The program of studies may stretch out for ten to fifteen years instead of four, but the same number of contact hours must be preserved. Otherwise the degree will be debased, the division will be dishonored, and the university will lose money.[9]

Despite this austere logic, counselors, administrators, and professors often find ways to temper application of the rules to students most seriously affected by them. Course options are allowed, a generous interpretation is made of transcripts of credit from other institutions, and instructors enter into various informal agreements with students. In the full-scale evening colleges, the program can be focused somewhat more directly on the needs of mature students than is the case in other situations. But the general pattern for the degree remains fixed; a timid or rigid staff member who wants to follow it rigorously is supported not merely by the letter of the regulations but also by the weight of university opinion.

The more independent evening colleges and university extension divisions have also served as incubators for new programs

[8] J. T. Carey, *Forms and Forces in University Adult Education* (Chicago: Center for the Study of Liberal Education for Adults, 1961), pp. 228–229.

[9] Ninety-six percent of the evening colleges "report that year in and year out their income is greater than their expenditures. The amounts seem to depend upon the size of the college and upon the way individual university auditors figure 'profit.'" J. Dyer, *Ivory Towers in the Market Place* (Indianapolis: Bobbs-Merrill, 1956), p. 43.

designed to meet community needs, some of which grew into degree sequences and established separate status within the institution. While the histories of such efforts take many specific forms, a general pattern of development is clear. A dean of extension becomes aware that a cluster of people in the community—usually an occupational group—needs systematic training. He develops first one course, then several, then a sequence. Initially the students are undereducated adult practitioners, but gradually the program attracts people who want to enter the occupation. At some point, the sequence of courses is sufficiently advanced to become either the heart of an independent degree-granting college or a field of specialization within an existing one. At Columbia University, to give but one example, the extension division was instrumental in helping to found the School of Business, the School of Dentistry, the program in optometry, the School of Dramatic Arts, the program in graphic arts, and the School of Painting and Sculpture.[10] In each of these cases and in uncounted others, an internal degree program was significantly shaped by the external teaching arm of the university.

We can therefore roughly distinguish two forms of extension degrees, though countless subtleties of differentiation exist. In the first, a special degree has been organized, paralleling that offered within the normal institutional framework but separately structured and administered. An adequately large range of courses from the university program is offered to make it possible for adults to complete all their work within the extension framework. In the second form, an external course of studies is nurtured (often to fulfill some community need) and may eventually evolve into an internal degree. In both cases, whatever the variation of content and method, the basic pattern of the degree as it evolved in the last quarter of the nineteenth century remains unchanged.

Adult Degree

The ridiculousness of treating experienced men and women learners as though they were still teen-agers was pointed out again

---

[10] J. A. Burrill, *A History of Adult Education at Columbia University* (New York: Columbia University Press, 1954).

and again from the very beginning of extension work.[11] Despite
continuing criticism, the effort to rethink the entire degree pattern
to make it conform with adult requirements did not make substantial headway until the post–World War II period. Partly in response
to the demands of returning veterans, universities began to realize
that to meet the urgent needs of their adult clientele they would
have to design wholly new patterns of degree requirements based
upon traditional aims but using new means.

The first major effort of this sort occurred in university
schools of business, sometimes in collaboration with extension divisions and evening colleges. Such schools were confronted with men
who wanted degrees but who had already been seasoned by military
and civilian administration; they revolted against instruction presenting management and the organization of personnel and materials as unfamiliar concepts. These sophisticates had, as directors of
complex enterprises, achieved a status which campus students would
not reach until years after graduation. The older group was interested in such problems as the effective use of overall fiscal controls,
the nature of governmental influence on business, and the processes
of supervision—not in the rudiments of accounting, marketing, and
production. New baccalaureate and M.B.A. programs based on
broad and deep content and scheduled to fit into the lifestyle of the
businessman began to appear, some of them sponsored by prestigious
universities.

Soon general efforts were made to free the adult student from
the restrictions imposed by the internal degree and the established
forms of the extension degree. One effort was centered on exempting
such students from taking all the orthodox courses. In the early
1950s, Columbia announced a new plan, developed in part by Jack N.
Arbolino and Ewald B. Nyquist, by which students could establish
through performance on examinations the right to work for a degree
(and even be exempt from some collegiate course requirements)
without a high school diploma. Brooklyn College developed another
form of advanced standing which received a great deal of attention; it established a system by which faculty evaluators could free

[11] A particularly eloquent statement of this view may be found in
J. S. Diekhoff, *The Domain of the Faculty in Our Expanding Colleges* (New
York: Harper and Row, 1956).

a student from some curricular obligations based on their estimate of what he had learned from experience. Soon many colleges and universities were experimenting along the same general lines.

In the 1960s, a major new development became evident: a degree, usually a baccalaureate, completely designed with the needs of adults in mind. While the deans of extension divisions and evening colleges often took the lead in initiating such degrees, the eventual pattern of requirements was worked out carefully with full involvement of university decision-making bodies. At the University of Oklahoma, for example, the process took four years and included a year-long seminar by thirty faculty members and administrators; two years of discussion by a faculty committee which finally recommended the establishment of a Bachelor of Liberal Studies and a College of Continuing Education to provide it; and consideration and eventual approval of these recommendations by the Extension Council, the Council on Instruction, the University Regents, and the State Regents for Higher Education. Similar processes occurred on other campuses, and soon programs were under way at other institutions of which the most widely publicized have been Syracuse University, Roosevelt University, Goddard College, Brigham Young University, and the University of South Florida.

While each such program has evolved as a result of thought and practice on the sponsoring campus, the dominant theme is that education should be fitted to the concerns and lifestyle of the mature student who is active in the normal affairs of adulthood. The Oklahoma program may serve as an example. Its objectives are clearly defined but are no different from those which might be established for an internal liberal arts degree. The curriculum is built on the theme "Man in the Twentieth Century" and contains three broad areas of study—humanities, social sciences, and natural sciences—as well as a subsequent effort to integrate the three areas. The curriculum is centered on, though not circumscribed by, the student's mastery of approximately 130 key books from a periodically revised list.

The methods are suited to varied adult ways of life. While the central emphasis is on reading, students are guided into many other activities available in their communities. Each person moves as rapidly or slowly as his wishes and circumstances allow. Each student has a professor or a mentor who helps plan and guide a personal program of independent study. Intensive residential seminars lasting three to four weeks are also offered, and attendance at some of them is required. When the student feels he is ready to do so, he takes a comprehensive examination in each area of study. Each student, with the guidance of a faculty advisor, must prepare a paper reporting his in-depth study of a specialized subject. When the student has passed the examinations, performed successfully in several seminars, and completed his study, he is awarded the degree. A special schedule of fees brings the total cost to the student to $2150. The 2618 students registered in the Oklahoma program in 1971 were resident in all states and the District of Columbia, in fourteen foreign countries, and in numerous armed-service bases abroad.[12]

Bold though such an adult-degree pattern may be, it usually adheres to certain traditions. It is sponsored by a regular degree-granting institution. Though it often grows up under the sponsorship of an extension division or evening college and may still have close ties with its parent, it usually achieves independence as a school or college. It involves the customary functions of admission, instruction, and evaluation. Control of the program is kept in the hands of a teaching faculty. The methods of learning are fairly conventional, based on reading, tutorial guidance, and discussion. And the student's accomplishment is measured by performance on written or oral examination or by demonstrated competence in writing and discussion.

New Conceptions

The discussion of the external degree which began in late 1970 did not accept any of these traditional elements as unalterable. Some people, at least, seemed ready to accept one or all of the following ideas: elimination of admission requirements; granting of degrees by government bureaus, associations, or other nonuniversity organizations; creation of new institutions designed solely to award

---

[12] This description of the Oklahoma program is taken from the much longer account of it provided in R. Troutt, *Special Degree Programs for Adults* (Iowa City, American College Testing Program, 1971).

the external degree; granting of degrees by evaluative (nonteaching) institutions; assumption of the major teaching load by non-faculty, part-time people; use of unconventional methods of learning and teaching (television, audiotapes, videotapes, programed instruction, learning modules, work-study programs, computerized instruction, undirected experience); demonstration and evaluation of accomplishment by a variety of innovative means both formal and informal (possibly including the judgment of a mentor or committee that a student had undergone a set of experiences undertaken for noneducational reasons; for example, a student at one institution received advanced standing in a sociology sequence on the ground that she had lived all her life in a city slum).

These bold suggestions make it clear that a watershed has been reached. In the past, the external degree has been in large measure, to use W. Todd Furniss' phrase, "the extension of extension."[13] But proposals now being made go to the very heart of the system of higher education and call for radical changes in its structure and processes.

Even in relatively conventional and well-established situations where there is no thought of undertaking the more extreme proposals just suggested, non-traditional curricula are being developed. A third of all American colleges and universities are probably now engaged in truly unconventional programs, according to a study of the supply of non-traditional education conducted in the spring of 1972 by the Center for Research and Development in Higher Education for the Commission on Non-Traditional Study. Of some 351 non-traditional programs analyzed in detail because they were identified by institutional respondents (typically senior academic administrators) as ones "likely to receive the greatest resources and support," 112 award the baccalaureate and 67 the associate degree. Table 1 shows the curricular options allowed students in these programs as checked on the survey questionnaire. The results show no clear-cut pattern of change. Non-traditional features such as learning contracts and multicampus study are mixed with such traditional elements as required concentration and distribution of courses. Indeed, contrary movements are evident in com-

[13] W. T. Furniss, *Degrees for Nontraditional Students* (Washington, D.C.: American Council on Education, 1971).

Table 1

CURRICULAR OPTIONS OR REQUIREMENTS IN
NON-TRADITIONAL UNDERGRADUATE DEGREE PROGRAM

Options or Requirements	Percentage of Programs	
	Bachelor (N = 112)	Associate (N = 67)
Students may begin program at any time (not only start of term)	29	24
Students design own programs	48	13
Most or all of curriculum structured or prescribed	33	66
Learning contracts between students and faculty	42	22
Concentration or major required	51	25
Distribution among courses (general education) required	40	43
Pacing of program individually determined	63	54
Course work at different campuses possible	47	25
Students may earn degree or complete program on part-time basis	60	73
No information	1	0

NOTE: Special tabulation provided by Janet Ruyle, Center for Research and Development, University of California, Berkeley.

plete prescription of courses in some programs and complete freedom for students to select courses in others.

As subsequent pages show, this same diversity of approach characterizes the whole external-degree movement. Perhaps the only common characteristic at present is a desire to open up the academic system and provide a wide diversity of options for a student body no longer made up exclusively of young postadolescents.

Definitions and Distinctions

Even at this early stage, however, it is possible to begin the task of definition and the drawing of distinctions. An *external* degree is one awarded to an individual on the basis of some program of preparation (devised either by himself or by an educational institution) which is not centered on traditional patterns of residential collegiate or university study. Essentially this definition is a negative one which, in simplest terms, says that an external degree is not an internal degree.

The positive definition of such a degree is based on a conception of the needs of its clients. The *extension* degree centers on the belief that a man or woman living in the community requires the same kind of program as the postadolescent living on the campus. The extension degree may be shaped initially for either audience, but it is then extended in substantially identical form to the other. The *adult* degree is focused directly on the nature of the mature person and the lifestyle he or she follows. While there are resemblances between the internal degree and the adult degree as far as both ends and means are concerned, the two are essentially different since they are based on the needs of people at different stages of life. (A variant of the adult degree can, however, become an internal degree, as is now happening on an experimental basis at the University of Oklahoma.) The new and extreme (in the United States) conceptions of the external degree have not yet become sufficiently clear to permit their essential natures to be defined, but major current approaches are explored in Chapter Four. Some efforts have been made to devise positive names. Thus, Stephen K. Bailey has suggested "flexible time/space higher education,"[14] a term which, however descriptive, may not pass into common speech. When it is necessary hereafter to distinguish the new ventures from extension and adult degrees, they are called *assessment* degrees, though this term is no more than a convention adopted for the sake of convenience. As various programs develop, they probably can be grouped logically into clusters, each with a name of its own.[15] The term *external* degree then may grow less and less widely used and finally have only historical significance.

[14] S. K. Bailey, "Flexible Time-Space Programs: A Plea for Caution," in D. W. Vermilye (Ed.), *The Expanded Campus: Current Issues in Higher Education 1972* (San Francisco: Jossey-Bass, 1972), pp. 172–173. This classification is briefly described in Chapter Four.

[15] A first attempt to identify such clusters has been made by J. Valley, "External Degree Programs," in S. B. Gould and K. P. Cross (Eds.), *Explorations in Non-Traditional Study* (San Francisco, Jossey-Bass, 1972).

In both old and new forms of the external degree, the target audience has been adults; but the potential market is a large one. Let us focus for the moment on the baccalaureate. The Bureau of the Census estimated that in March 1971, 38,029,000 Americans twenty-five years of age or over had completed high school but not gone beyond it. Of these people, 20,632,000 were under forty-five years of age. The vast majority probably has no desire or need for further education, but some certainly do; in fact many may well have learned a great deal of college-level content by various informal means. An unknown number of persons who have not completed high school might also be interested and capable of securing an external degree, and research suggests that it may be possible to recruit a substantial number of people from this group. The most promising category is those people who have already signified an interest in college study and some aptitude for it but who, for some reason, have not yet completed degree work. The Bureau of the Census estimated that, in March 1971, 11,782,000 persons twenty-five years of age and over had completed from one to three years of college. Of these people, 6,465,000 were under forty-five years of age.[16]

An important second audience (but one about which much debate has occurred) is made up of young people aged seventeen through twenty-one who, if they were to go to college, would normally take an internal degree. Should they be allowed the option of an external degree instead? Many people believe that if the answer is no, many able students will be denied the right to higher education, this denial falling most heavily upon women, the poor, the geographically isolated, and the members of minority racial and ethnic groups. Others believe that if the answer is yes, the quality of degrees will decline, many colleges and universities which offer only internal degrees will be forced to close, and many unqualified young people will be encouraged to undertake programs which are meaningless for them. Since these and other issues are discussed at length in the final two chapters of this book, they are not detailed here.

[16] The figures in this paragraph were calculated from data presented in *Educational Attainment, 1971,* Series P–20, No. 229 (Washington, D.C.: U.S. Bureau of the Census, 1971).

A third audience, paradoxically enough, may well be made up eventually of those who take an internal degree which has been strongly influenced by activities originally developed and perfected in external degree programs. As has already been noted, some extension degrees have first been developed for adults in the community and later been provided for postadolescents on the campus. Perhaps the same kind of transfer will continue to occur as new forms of external degrees are perfected. Even more likely is the borrowing or adaptation into internal-degree sequences of special features of new programs, such as the bold new methods of teaching and testing suggested in some of the non-traditional proposals. Why should such options be open to a twenty-six-year old but not to a nineteen-year old?

Many educators believe, in fact, that the greatest effect of the external degree will be its influence upon the internal degree. In the last fifty years, college and university faculties have spent a vast amount of time on curriculum revision. A special study group supported by the Hazen Foundation came to the conclusion that "the harsh truth is that all this activity is generally a waste of time."[17] While few people might reach so drastic a conclusion, the current literature on reforming the undergraduate curriculum is not especially optimistic.[18] Perhaps this innovative effort needs to be shifted to another setting, one which is not heavily influenced by the closed systems of recurrent routines. Perhaps the best hope for the future lies in experimental programs aimed at new clienteles in community settings—programs which use unconventional methods and in which failure does not have drastic and permanent consequences for both student and sponsoring institution. The external degree allows its sponsors the freedom to be flexible; the result may well be the emergence of new goals and processes which will enrich all higher education.

[17] *The Student in Higher Education* (New Haven, Conn.: Hazen Foundation, 1968).

[18] See, for example, J. Harvey, *Reforming the Undergraduate Curriculum: Problems and Proposals* (Washington, D.C.: Eric Clearinghouse on Higher Education, 1971, ED 048 518).

Foreign External-
Degree Programs

Foreigners are contemporary posterity.

MADAME DE STAEL

*T*he people of the United States may soon grow familiar with new ways of securing baccalaureate and advanced degrees—ways which are novel in this country but ancient and familiar elsewhere in the world. The purpose of this chapter is not to explore every variation of practice now followed abroad (some of which are bizarre or trivial), but to describe briefly some of the programs and institutions which are relevant to the American situation, focusing chiefly on England where much thought has been given to the external degree.

Basic Procedures

Any comprehensive history of the university as an institution discusses its rise as an ecclesiastical corporation and, after long centuries, its slow secularization. The right to award degrees was granted initially by a charter issued by a pope, an archbishop, or other religious authority, or by a sovereign government based on the divine right of the ruler. The institution which gradually evolved, though its roots can be found in early charters, carries out five formal procedures marking the progress of an individual from his point of entry into the system of higher education until he is fully entitled to practice a profession. These five formal procedures are: enforcement of admission (or matriculation) requirements, provision of instruction, evaluation of the individual's competence in the content taught, awarding of the certificate or degree, and licensure to practice a profession. An individual may move through this series several times in cycles or subcycles; and some of these procedures may be linked in intricate ways, omitted, or lose their sharp identity. Ordinarily, however, each procedure is formally distinguishable from the others.

In American practice, all five have become part of a single continuous process and, with the exception of licensure, are generally accepted as the work of a college or university. Even licensure by the state to practice a profession is tied to the system of higher education when only those who hold degrees from an accredited institution are admitted to the government-conducted examinations. The closest link in the process is between teaching and evaluation. In the United States, the professor usually grades his own students, and the degree is generally awarded on a summation of credits based on the grades of a number of professors.

But in English practice (out of one small sector of which the American college grew), the five procedures are, and have always been, readily separable from and independent of one another, contributing to the conditions which made the external degree not only possible but necessary in England. Thus, if it wished, an ecclesiastical authority could grant degrees directly rather than setting up a university for that purpose. In 1534, for instance, as an early consequence of the separation of the English church from Papal authority, the Archbishop of Canterbury was given the right to grant surrogate degrees in any subject matter he wished. This privilege was broadened; and eventually many different bodies were created to prepare students for licensure, with the University's work being centered on scholarly study.[1]

[1] W. H. G. Armytage, "The Universities of Britain," in *Common-*

In the English pattern of higher education developed by the first half of the nineteenth century, instruction was divorced from evaluation and the awarding of credentials. At Oxford and Cambridge, the colleges taught and the universities examined. Walter Bagehot observed that "if you want a university which is trusted without suspicion to decide the result of tuition . . . you must not let it begin to interfere in tuition."[2] And a faith in external, generalized examinations—as used for testing applicants to colleges, for admission to the civil service and for assessing the relative accomplishment of schools by measuring the knowledge of their students[3] —forecast the concern for evaluation and assessment which was to occur in the United States a hundred years later.

University of London External Degree

The form taken by the University of London at its establishment in 1836 was, therefore, virtually inevitable. Two separate and antagonistic colleges had recently come into being; their differences were identified succinctly by a Royal Commission three-quarters of a century later: "When University College was founded in 1826, . . . it was intended to be a university for those who were unable to enter the national universities of Oxford and Cambridge either because they lacked the means or because they were at that time excluded on the ground of their religious belief. But there were many persons of influence who regarded it as essential to maintain the theological doctrines of the Church of England as a fundamental part of university instruction, and who yet shared the desire of the founders of University College to provide university education for those who could not afford to go to Oxford or Cambridge. This led to the foundation of King's College which began its instruction in 1831."[4] The antagonism between these two young colleges was

---

wealth Universities Yearbook, 1971 (London: Association of Commonwealth Universities, 1971), p. 125.

[2] Quoted in E. Ashby, *Universities: British, Indian, African* (Cambridge, Mass.: Harvard University Press, 1966), p. 25.

[3] For a general account of the rise of comprehensive examination systems in England during this period see R. J. Montgomery, *Examinations: An Account of Their Evolution as Administrative Devices in England* (Pittsburgh: University of Pittsburgh Press, 1965).

[4] Royal Commission on University Education in London, *Final Re-*

so great that they could not be brought together, the backers of each were so powerful that neither could be given the right to award degrees without conferring that right on the other, and yet nobody felt it appropriate to give such a right to both.

The eventual result was the creation in 1836 of a separate body, the University of London, to conduct examinations and to confer degrees. Despite its title, the new institution was a government bureau: the members of its senate were appointed by the Privy Council; the Treasury was directly responsible for any deficit; the staff was made up of civil servants and their clerks; and Parliament made detailed inquiries into both procedures and finances. The new institution, said the Haldane Commission, was "an examining board with the title of the University of London."[5]

The plan was simple. The candidate for a degree must matriculate, meeting the usual requirements for doing so. Before being admitted to the examination, he must produce a certificate showing that he had followed a course of instruction at one of the two London colleges or at some other institution approved by the Privy Council. This latter right was greatly broadened by a Supplemental Charter of 1849 which allowed candidates to study at institutions anywhere in the British Empire or the "territories under the government of the East India Company." These institutions were not necessarily accredited themselves, and the University of London had no right of inspection over them. Eventually they included not merely the ancient universities of England and the Universities of Toronto and Sydney, but also such organizations as the Protestant Dissenters' College at Rotherham, the Workingmen's College at London, and various medical schools attached to hospitals.

The number of institutions accepted became so great and so meaningless in its variety that, as Douglas Logan, a recent historian of the university, notes, a new charter granted in 1858 "quietly dispensed with requirement of attendance at an approved institution, and thereafter the university accepted as candidates all who presented themselves for examination, provided of course that they had passed the matriculation examination and had paid their

---

port (London: His Majesty's Stationery Office, 1913), p. 3. This Commission and its Report are usually given the name of its chairman, Lord Haldane, and will be so designated here.

[5] *Final Report,* p. 3.

fees."[6] Thus the London External Degree came into being; it remained the only degree of the University until 1900 when, as the eventual result of twenty-five years of increasing pressure, the institution began to admit students and provide instruction to them. But the new and much fuller program did not crowd out the older one. As a recent leaflet from the institution notes, while London "has developed during the last hundred years into the largest teaching university in the United Kingdom, it has continued to fulfill its original purpose as an examining body for external students of whom there are now (1970) approximately thirty-five thousand."[7]

While a man or woman independently engaged in private study for a degree has long been the dominant image of the external student, the system which made such study possible also discharged a second function of great importance. The University of London served as guide and counselor for a number of other institutions of higher learning until they gained sufficient strength to attain university status and award their own degrees. Every university institution established in England and Wales between 1836 and 1949 went through an apprenticeship during which its students were prepared for London external degrees. In addition, the University of London aided the movement toward colonial independence by setting up so-called special relationships with budding colonial colleges so that they could eventually grant degrees of their own rather than depend on London external degrees. The influence of the program extended to Africa, Asia, and the Caribbean and, while in existence, did a great deal to provide new nations with the leaders they required. Finally, the University of London itself provided a model to be copied elsewhere; later in this chapter, several such institutional copies will be mentioned.

The London degree for external students, as it has evolved after a century and a half of experience, is often described in simple terms but is in actuality a highly complex phenomenon only quickly sketched here. (It is well to remember the remark once made by an American and quoted, though without approval, by London's

[6] D. Logan, *The University of London* (London: Athlone Press, 1962), p. 11.

[7] "The External System of the University of London," unprinted memorandum, ref. ER/R/MTT/216. (London: University of London, n.d.).

vice-chancellor: "It is probable that any reasonably intelligent man, if he will exert himself sufficiently, can arrive at an understanding of the organization of the University of London: that he can eventually discover what things the University does, what are the degrees of affiliation of its various subsidiary branches, what is the relationship between the parts of the cumbersome whole. It is equally probable that no intelligent person will take that trouble unless there exists some vital necessity for him to do so.")[8]

To begin with, there is not one degree but a cluster of them including the Bachelor of Arts, the Bachelor of Divinity, the Bachelor of Science, the Bachelor of Laws, the Master of Arts, the Master of Philosophy, the Doctor of Philosophy, the Doctor of Literature, and the Bachelors of Medicine, Surgery, and Dental Surgery. The University also offers diplomas and certificates in such fields as education, library and information sciences, public administration, and social studies.

The range of content in which students can be examined is very broad. The curriculum for the B.A. General Degree includes fifty-nine subjects, whereas that for the B.Sc. General Degree includes eighteen. In addition, specialized B.Sc. degrees are offered in such fields as engineering, economics, and sociology. The British make a distinction between a Pass degree and one awarded with Honors (First Class; Second Class, Upper Division; Second Class, Lower Division; and Third Class). Both kinds can be secured externally at London. The requirements for various degrees differ substantially from one another in provisions for both matriculation and examination; and, as at any vital university, regulations change frequently so that students must constantly keep up-to-date on them. In general, the aspiration of the University is to make "most of its degrees available alike to internal and external students. In some fields the syllabuses and examination papers are identical for both, although this is now less common than formerly. The principal guarantee of equivalence of standard is that the same academic authorities are responsible for the preparation and approval of syllabuses for internal and external students and for the conduct of their examinations. There are either common boards of examiners or,

[8] Logan, p. 1.

where the examinations differ, interlocking appointments ensure that the majority of the examiners of external students are University teachers who examine internal students."[9]

The University's announcements suggest that once the student has decided what degree or diploma he wishes to pursue, his course of action follows a simple and well-marked pathway. He demonstrates his eligibility for admission, indicates the subjects in which he wishes to be examined and the dates he will present himself for examination; then he proceeds to his studies. After the passage of a due period of time (the University sets a minimum but no maximum), he presents himself for examination (either on the date originally indicated or on another to which he has been allowed to change). If he fails, he tries again and, in practice, is permitted to do so as often as necessary. The examinations can be taken at many centers in the United Kingdom and overseas, though oral or practical examinations must be taken in London.

An elaborate structure of teaching activities has been built up (largely outside the University) to support this system of admission and evaluation. The University divides its external students into two groups: those taking formal courses at a community institution offering a preparatory curriculum for a degree and private students who study on their own or with the help of a proprietary correspondence course. The University will not advise students on the merits of any of the schools which offer preparation for external-degree examinations. As for generalized guidance, it is assumed that the students in the first group will be advised by the counselors at the institutions they attend; an External Advisory Service has been established to help private students adjust to the program studied. The Service also arranges short courses during the Easter and summer vacations, concentrating on subjects in which the external student might have difficulty gaining access to needed facilities. Sometimes a postgraduate student is also assigned an adviser to serve as guide or mentor.

The number of students in both categories has been rising rapidly in recent years, growing from twenty-five thousand to thirty-five thousand between 1962 and 1970. It is assumed that the Na-

[9] "The External System," p. 1.

tional Council on Academic Awards and the Open University (both of which will be described later) will cause a decrease in external-degree enrollment at the University of London. A recent publication of the latter notes dryly that "the University . . . welcomes the relief which it hopes that the two other bodies . . . may afford."

The failure rate for external students is much higher than it is for internal students, and University authorities believe that it "is largely due to the tendency shown by external students to enter for examinations without allowing adequate time for preparation. A student is, therefore, strongly advised not to seek early entry to his examinations, but to wait until he has fully mastered the whole of the syllabus before making the attempt."[10] Overall, 71 percent of the United Kingdom candidates are successful as contrasted with 47 percent of those who take their examinations overseas. Despite this failure rate, the number of graduates is still substantial, as shown in Table 2.

The cost of the program to the student is relatively modest and is based on registration and examination fees. If he undertook instruction at a community institution or private correspondence school, its fees would have to be added; but the extra out-of-pocket costs of an external degree would probably be far less than those of securing an internal degree. The correspondence schools, incidentally, have achieved important status in the system. Several concentrate on preparing students for external degrees.

From the beginning, the external degree has experienced bitter opposition. It was born as a result of religious controversy. It was attacked as a separation of instruction from examination. It did not require the acculturating (some would say the civilizing)' effect of a full-time collegial experience. It fitted learning into the nooks and crannies of life rather than treating it as a central and absorbing experience. For a century and a half, revolts and attacks have been mounted against it, particularly and with great directness by the Haldane Commission in its 1913 report. Some of its comments are so relevant to the American experience they are quoted in Chapter Six.

But in the United Kingdom, the Empire, and the Common-

[10] *General Information for External Students* (London: University of London, 1971).

Table 2

EXTERNAL DEGREES AND CERTIFICATES AWARDED
BY UNIVERSITY OF LONDON, 1970

	United Kingdom		Overseas[a]	
	Candidates	Degrees Awarded	Candidates	Degrees Awarded
First degrees	4,981	3,547	277	131
Master's degrees	107	60	26	8
Ph.D. degrees	155	111	...	...
Undergraduate diplomas	239	183	18	8
Postgraduate diplomas	799	602	54	14

[a] Indicates where the examination was held, not the country of origin of the candidate.
Source: "The External System," pp. 3–4.

wealth, the degree met an important need. It was treated with contempt by a few and given second-class status by many; but the need and demand for it were so great that even its opponents usually recommended (as did the Haldane Commission) not that it be abandoned, but that at some indeterminate date it be gradually phased out of existence. At home, it gave to determined and able members of the lower-middle and lower classes their only chance for a university education. Abroad, it helped educate leaders for colonies moving toward independence. It has been said, perhaps with more hyperbole than truth, that the two essentials for the prime ministership of such a nation are a London external degree and a period of residence in an English jail.

When the Haldane Commission report was reviewed for implementation thirteen years after its issuance, the delay caused chiefly by World War I, the inspectorial committee began its examination of the University by considering the external degree. Its conclusions were firm and absolute:

> *As a result of discussion and inquiry we found not only that no member of the Committee contemplated the*

*abolition of degree examinations for external students, but
also that no responsible body desired to give evidence in
that sense. In the circumstances we decided to make known
our views and we therefore informed the University that we
did not wish anyone to spend time and labour in preparing
evidence on the general question of the continuance of the
system of examinations for external students, because "in
the view of the whole Committee these examinations have
in the past served, and will in the future serve, a useful purpose." We may add that evidence subsequently submitted to
us disclosed no demand, or indeed support, for the abolition
of these examinations. In view of our terms of reference and
the proposals of the Haldane Commisison we have heard
evidence as to the scope of these examinations, and we may
say here that none of our recommendations is in any way
designed to restrict the present facilities available for external students or to prevent their development.*[11]

However, this vehement endorsement of the external degree
by the Committee did not settle matters in England. Some English
educators even assert, by the way, that no "external" degree exists,
since all London applicants must meet the same matriculation requirements and pass the same examinations. This argument places
full weight on entrance and exit procedures and pays no attention
to the essential element of instruction.

As the United States begins to have substantial experience
with non-traditional forms of external degrees, many of the British
arguments will be repeated across the Atlantic. In the review of
current issues in Chapters Five and Six, therefore, further reference
is made to the University of London experience and particularly
to the perennial controversies which have been so prominent a part
of its existence.

Birkbeck College Adult Degree

To classify Birkbeck College of the University of London is
difficult for, in a very real sense, it is unique. A full-scale college

[11] Board of Education, *Report of the Departmental Committee on the
University of London* (London: His Majesty's Stationery Office, 1926), p. 8.

with its own distinguished faculty and handsome and extensive physical facilities, it offers instruction in twenty-one subjects in the arts and sciences, and it awards a full range of both Pass and Honors baccalaureate and graduate degrees. From the outside, its instructional patterns appear very similar to those of the typical English university. But both the history of the College and its present ethos make it similar to the adult-degree programs in American universities, though the institution has a power and authority transcending anything yet achieved in the United States.

The College was founded (as the London Mechanics Institution) by George Birkbeck in 1823 as a way to help workingmen achieve an education "in the principles of the arts they practice, and in the various branches of science and useful knowledge." After a long independent career, often marked by vicissitudes, the institution was suggested by the Haldane Commission in 1913 as the instrument by which the University of London could best carry out what the Commission regarded as the very necessary function of providing university instruction for part-time students. The Commission was wholehearted in its support of the idea. It argued that "in a city of the size of London there is a number of men and women rather older than the average student, with a keen desire for learning, whose circumstances prevent them from devoting their whole day to study, and for whose needs the University should make provision. They will need great patience and strength of purpose, if they are to receive from evening study the same kind of training that the full-time student receives. At the best they will lose something which those who are more fortunate will get. But while they may suffer from the pressure of material cares, we are assured that they gain immensely from their zeal, their experience of life, and the maturity of their intellectual development."[12]

Nor did the Commission believe that restricted provisions would suffice for part-time students:

> *We believe the attempt to give them an education as good as that offered by the University to its day students is well worth making. It is an experiment that has never yet*

[12] *Final Report,* p. 31.

been carried out consistently, and one that must prove more expensive than provision for work of the same character in the daytime, but we think the University of the metropolis should undertake it. The chief teachers engaged in this work should do no class teaching in the daytime; they should have the same qualifications as the other professors of the University; like University teachers they should be appointed by the University; they should receive the same salaries, and have the use of libraries and laboratories as well equipped as those available for day teaching. It is of the greatest importance that the laboratories, and especially those for more advanced work, should be reserved exclusively for evening students, so that apparatus they have set up should not be shifted or disarranged to make room for day students. This arrangement will be relatively more costly than day instruction, for the laboratories and apparatus will for the most part not be available in the daytime; but if evening students are really to be given the same advantages as those provided for the ordinary day students, it is necessary.[13]

Under the general terms set forward, Birkbeck College (which had for many years prepared students for the external degree) was made a school of the University in 1920 and was incorporated by royal charter in 1926. It has remained predominantly a college for part-time students; in 1969–1970, there were 2001 of them, 1385 men and 616 women. It is now possible for full-time students to attend Birkbeck; in the same year, there were 379 full-time students, 266 men and 113 women. In 1968–1969, 392 degrees were awarded, 236 bachelor's (6 Pass and 230 with Honors), 114 master's, and 42 doctorates.[14]

A student at Birkbeck is required to meet the usual standards for admission to a British university, though some alternative arrangements (all of them fairly demanding) have been established, presumably to take account of the varied backgrounds of mature students. Fees are assessed on an annual basis and vary

[13] *Final Report,* p. 32.
[14] *Commonwealth Universities Yearbook, 1971* (London: Association of Commonwealth Universities, 1971).

markedly with the course taken and whether the student is full-time or part-time. The charges for overseas students are substantially higher than for residents of the United Kingdom.

In 1967, the master of Birkbeck spoke of the isolation which accompanies his College's eminence. "We know very well," he said, "that we have yet to convince the other universities that this is a good formula and meets an important public need. There are no other Birkbecks, and part-time degree studies are not in the front line of advance anywhere, to our knowledge." These words seem remarkable, particularly since they were spoken soon after the creation of the Council for National Academic Awards (CNAA) and while the idea of the Open University was being introduced. But the master had something special in mind when he spoke of part-time education:

> *We are frank propagandists, and should be offended if anyone thought that we maintained judicial impartiality about the questions discussed. We believe that Birkbeck's answer to these questions—how to give mature, working students a university education—is the best answer available, though it is not often imitated. We talk about the Birkbeck "faith," because we can offer no empirical proof that the answer is the best. The faith is simply this: that mature, part-time students are fully capable of degree work as demanding as that faced by school-leavers; that they need, within the university, their own college, where they are the real cocks of the walk; that their college needs its own specialist academic staff, which must be at least as good as at any other college; that this implies a high level of research and postgraduate training, for which the mature student is in any case well suited; and that the curriculum, though founded on the solid core of established disciplines, must also be venturesome and experimental, willing to reach out into new areas of development.*[15]

[15] F. K. Hare, "Preface," in *The University Education of Mature Students,* addresses given at the Birkbeck College Conference, July 20–22, 1967, pp. 4–5.

Council for National Academic Awards

A recent English book points out that, in that country, "apart from electronics and natural gas, higher education has grown faster than any major national enterprise in the 1960s."[16] Much of this expansion came about as a result of the 1963 report of the Robbins Committee, whose bold suggestions led to the enlargement of existing universities, the creation of new ones, the elevation of colleges of advanced technology to university status, and other major changes. In particular, the Committee recognized that many institutions not sufficiently broad in scope or rich in resources to be raised to university status nonetheless offered programs of a high academic level. Following what has been called "Robbins's golden rule" that "equal academic awards should be available for equal performance," the Committee concluded that "facilities must therefore be provided for those who do work of degree standard to obtain degrees, even if the institutions they attend have no independent power to award them."[17]

After paying its respects to the London external degree ("Whatever may be its future, its honourable place in academic history is a matter of common consent"[18]), the Committee developed the idea that some entirely new degree-awarding device was needed which could be more flexible than the University's arrangements, could relate evaluation closely to teaching, and could provide for a full range of pass, honours, and advanced degrees in a broad range of subjects. Such a system, it argued, was essential not merely for the equity it afforded to individuals but also to meet industrial and commercial needs. The Committee therefore recommended that the function of the National Council for Technological Awards, which had established a strong tradition of awarding Diplomas in Technology, should be broadened to that of a Council of National Academic Awards, a degree-granting government body which would

[16] R. Layard, J. King, and C. Moser, *The Impact of Robbins* (Harmondsworth, Middlesex: Penguin, 1969), p. 13.

[17] Great Britain Committee on Higher Education, *Higher Education* (London: Her Majesty's Stationery Office, 1963), p. 140.

[18] *Final Report,* p. 140.

establish standards for programs of various sorts and award appropriate degrees to those who completed them.

This recommendation was almost immediately put into effect. A royal charter was granted in 1964 conferring full degree-
awarding powers to the Council and transforming it into what has
since been called, though not officially, a "disseminated" university.
The Council's thirty members—whose honorary president is the
Duke of Edinburgh—are drawn from education, industry, and government. Some are appointed by the government and others are
coopted by the Council itself.[19] By December 1, 1971, about three
hundred fifty undergraduate and thirty-five graduate courses had
been approved, the majority of them at local polytechnic institutes or colleges, a group of institutions which make up part of the
English "further education" provisions, recent innovations which
have no exact American parallels.

The process for approval of a program is rigorous, and the
Council does a great deal of advisory work to help institutions
strengthen their programs. It has established and periodically revises
the guidelines which must be followed by its network of committees
and examining boards in scrutinizing courses requesting consideration. Some of the standards are highly specific; for example, since
the Council "feels that many theses are unnecessarily long and dif-
fuse," a maximum limit of forty thousand words is put on Ph.D.
theses in science and technology and a maximum limit of seventy
thousand words is put on such theses in the arts and social studies.
Generally, however, the standards are rather broad. Among them
is the assertion that "the Council believes that it is possible in most
courses to bring out in the teaching the fact that scientific method,
in the sense of a critical and sceptical approach to enquiry and a
readiness to test hypotheses, enters at many points into subjects of
the arts and social sciences and that equally the spirit of speculative
enquiry, the exercise of creative imagination, and the capacity for
making value judgments are important in the activities of the scien-
tist and technologist." The subject boards which apply these stan-

[19] All of the information here presented on the CNAA was supplied
by the organization itself and comes from various reports and pamphlets of
the Council.

dards and which serve on a voluntary basis do not take their task lightly. In 1969–1970, for example, of the 231 courses considered, 131 were approved, 76 were rejected, and 24 were held over for further consideration.

Most courses are concerned with specific fields of study and deal with occupational subjects such as chemical engineering, ceramics, estate management, or pharmacy. However, multiple-disciplined, arts, and social sciences courses are also available; among them are graphic arts, humanities, modern studies, music, and sociology. Some courses are full-time, some are part-time, and some are "sandwich" programs which fit periods of work and study together. Most of the latter are "thin sandwich" courses (which alternate periods of six months in college and six months at work) or "2:1:1" courses made up of two initial years of study, one of work, and a final year of study. An effort is made to integrate these periods into a unified educative experience. The Council believes that such courses "give the students the opportunity of applying in a work situation what they learn during their periods in college, and of seeing how industrial and commercial organizations operate. As their course progresses, they are able to carry out more responsible tasks in the firm, and in many cases they can make a useful contribution well before the end of their training periods." Special arrangements are made to provide individual research assistance for candidates for the master's and doctor's degrees.

The number of students served by the Council has grown rapidly, and it may well become the largest degree-granting institution in the United Kingdom. In 1970–1971, there were 23,615 students enrolled in first-degree programs, 244 students enrolled in special postgraduate courses leading to the master's degree, and 869 students enrolled (in either colleges or research and industrial establishments) for the master's or doctorate. Degrees conferred in 1970 included 698 baccalaureates in the arts; 2193 baccalaureates in science; 50 masters of science; 22 masters of philosophy; and 60 doctorates of philosophy. The CNAA awards six kinds of baccalaureates, four with honors (at the customary levels), an ordinary degree, and an ordinary degree with commendation. In addition, a program to award special diplomas, most of them at the postgraduate level, is being worked out.

The student of English higher education cannot help noting the resemblance between the activities of the CNAA and the pattern followed earlier by the External Department of the University of London in aiding university colleges both at home and abroad to grow to independent status. Will the same cycle be completed by the new institution? The Robbins report refers to "the uprush of self-respect and vitality that came to the former university colleges with their constitution as self-governing, degree-awarding bodies." Perhaps at some future time, particularly if the CNAA has done its work well, at least some of the colleges for whom it now awards degrees may be strong enough to win independent university status.

Open University

The CNAA program was designed chiefly to serve young people wishing to continue their higher education immediately after secondary school, though some provision has been made, particularly in part-time courses, for older students. The Open University (OU), on the other hand, is specifically designed for adults, particularly those employed full-time. (A change of policy, to be put in effect in 1974, is described subsequently.) Only men and women twenty-one years of age or older can enter, and a strong effort is made to reach working-class (or blue-collar) people for whom the University serves as a second chance for an earlier-missed opportunity. This emphasis arises in part from the fact that OU is a creation of the Labour party, advanced by Harold Wilson in the 1963 election campaign and further developed by Jennie Lee, a Labour party leader in her own right and the widow of Aneurin Bevan, once deputy leader of the party.

The emphasis on adult education came in part from the party's historic support of this field but was also reinforced by the recognition that designing the program solely for adults would lessen the threat to the child-and-youth-serving educational establishment and also would keep the new institution from being flooded with rejects from the old ones. In order to succeed, the new university needed the collaboration of a wide network of other institutions;[20]

[20] This aspect of the growth of the institution is described in J.

even prime ministerial power could not have created the necessary cooperation if the new degree-granting institution, created overnight on a very large scale and lacking a long developmental period of growth, had suddenly emerged as a competitor to the established universities for the same group of young students.

For some not-easily-defined reason, The Open University instantly became a worldwide topic of concern—pro and con— among both educators and the general public; public awareness increased as plans were made, when its charter was granted in 1969, and when its program began in 1971. Interest has been particularly keen in the United States. "So great has been the flow of visitors to this institution," John Valley observed in 1972, "that it is becoming a mark of distinction among American educators to be able to say that one has not visited the Open University."[21] Many visitors were eager to express their views, providing facts and impressions sometimes so much at odds that one gains the impression that their authors are blind men from Hindustan, not observers from the United States. The present account of OU will give only a few essentials, assuming that later developments will be reported fully in the press and interpreted in magazines.

In his inaugural address on July 23, 1969, the chancellor of the Open University, Lord Crowther, stated that the word *open* in the title of the university refers to people, methods, places, and ideas. With respect to the first of these, and in contrast to the strict requirements for matriculation characteristic of most British universities, no academic bars to admission were set by OU, though, in filling the 25,000 first-year places available in 1971 from among 40,817 applicants seeking to take 62,147 courses, some balancing occurred in terms of occupation, geographic distribution, clarity of purpose, and course desired. (One author put the matter this way: "A manual laborer from Yorkshire who wished to study science was almost sure of acceptance, for example, while a teacher from the London

Robinson, "The Open University as a Cooperative Enterprise." *Adult Education,* January 1972, *44,* 285–292.

[21] J. Valley, "External Degree Programs," in S. B. Gould and K. P. Cross (Eds.), *Explorations in Non-Traditional Study* (San Francisco: Jossey-Bass, 1972), p. 106.

area who was interested in arts would face strong competition for a place.")[22] Aside from such initial screening, the general rule is "first come, first served." The proportion of working-class applicants was lower than desired, and efforts—apparently meeting with some success—are being made to raise it.[23] The division by sex was 70 percent male and 30 percent female. To encourage openness of access, the program is heavily subsidized by the government and the fees to students are as low as possible.

As to openness of methods, Lord Crowther referred to the fact that OU students learn by many means. The original intention was to rely on teaching by television; now this has been supplemented by other means of instruction, among them background reading, correspondence teaching (including written assignments graded by a tutor or a computer), self-assessment tests, radio broadcasts, special counseling, and class instruction at study centers and one-week residential summer schools. Many other resources required for particular courses are used; among these, the science kits have received much favorable attention. Efforts are made to engage the best available talent to write and produce the diverse materials required for the program.

Openness of place is assured by the fact that OU has no teaching campus, only a set of buildings near the new city of Milton Keynes, a city which, as Lord Crowther observed, bears "two of the widest-ranging names in the history of English thought." The students' learning is done in their homes or in other settings appropriate to their normal lives. In addition, about 280 study centers (backed up by 12 regional centers) provide places near enough each student for study, counseling, review of radio or television programs, attendance at occasional courses and meetings, and association with fellow learners. The density of population in the United Kingdom—557 persons per square mile as contrasted with 58 in the United States—is one of the reasons for the success of OU, since it means that such centers are of easy access to everyone. The process of interaction among learners is carried on intensively at the sum-

[22] J. Walsh, "The Open University: Breakthrough for Britain?" *Science,* November 1971, *174,* 676.

[23] Americans will discover, however, that the *Prospectus* for OU is no easier to understand than their own university catalogs and will wonder how much luck working-class people would have in reading it.

mer residential classes and by an elaborate system involving students in determining the policies and practices of the entire institution. And, as the prospectus points out, "the wearing of University insignia—ties, badges, and scarves—can also stimulate contact between students, and registered students receive details about these."

Openness of ideas is presumably to be found in the curriculum, which is organized into six fields: arts, educational studies, mathematics, science, social sciences, and technology. A full-time faculty paid at the usual university scale and supported by many administrators, part-time teachers, and counselors as well as by specialists in the media of instruction has been brought together and is hard at work planning and carrying out the novel curriculum. One credit is given for a year's work in a subject; and courses are organized on the basis of breadth and difficulty into foundation, second, third, and fourth levels. The only undergraduate degree is the B.A.; without honours, it requires the completion of six courses; with honours, it requires eight. Higher degrees and special diplomas will be offered eventually. Some of the courses are based on conventional, standardized bodies of content; others have been devised especially for OU and, as already noted, much creative thought has gone into the development of special instructional materials. In fact, OU hopes it can recoup much of its cost by the sale of these materials in other countries.

OU is already far more complex than this summary implies, and nothing about its past suggests that it will grow simpler in the future. It has had the money, the governmental sanctions, the social support, and the administrative drive to establish a completely new national system of education—using familiar components, perhaps, but putting them together in a novel fashion and using the best available skill to design and develop each of the parts. Enough work is planned—for example, the development of advanced courses in the curriculum—to keep the staff busy for years; and it seems likely that OU, being large and complex, will constantly encounter problems with its students, its collaborators, its opponents, and the government. In time, OU may become less rigid than its present lock-step arrangement now permits—at least it appears rigid to an outsider. Also, it may find more flexible ways "to act as a catalyst for a general increase in the transferability of credit." Beginning in 1974, OU will admit each year five hundred students between the ages of eighteen and twenty-one, half of whom will have standard university entrance qualifications and half of whom will not. The results of this experiment will be watched very closely since it will be interpreted as bringing OU into direct competition with the universities and the CNAA and as testing the established standards of entrance. Life will not be dull at the headquarters of this new institution, particularly since many will continue to keep a close and careful score on its successes and failures.

University of London Imitators

The University of London had profound influence in other countries as a model during the days of the British Empire. (The history of the London external degree is brilliantly described in the already-cited book by Eric Ashby.) In India, to cite an early example, the universities of Calcutta, Bombay, and Madras were founded on the University of London pattern in 1857 as regulating and examining bureaus. Very much later, they began to accept students, but only at the postgraduate level. As other Indian universities developed, the pattern changed somewhat. By the beginning of 1969, there were seventy-six institutions; and the number is still rising. Of the seventy-six, twenty-four concentrated on teaching, while fifty-two served primarily to establish standards and to administer examinations. In the latter, teaching was performed but was less significant than the "affiliating" role of governing the work of about three thousand colleges and special institutes. M. V. Mathur, the distinguished Indian educator, has pointed out that "the predominantly affiliating character of Indian universities is normally not found in many other parts of the world. Even today, most teachers do not participate in the formulation of curricula. Nor are most of them involved in setting the examinations for their students."[24]

It must be stressed, however, that while this system provides external degrees in one sense, it allows little provision for them in

[24] M. V. Mathur, "Tasks of Universities in India," in S. D. Kertesz (Ed.), *The Task of Universities in a Changing World* (Notre Dame, Ind.: University of Notre Dame Press, 1971), p. 471.

another. Virtually all students in India are full-time day students. The opportunity for part-time or independent study as a means of securing a degree is, for all practical purposes, absent; and there are few extension divisions, evening colleges, or correspondence courses at a university level. The creation of such opportunities has been strongly recommended as has the establishment of an open university, but such ventures have not thrived. In 1965–1966, about three-fourths of all Indian students were enrolled in arts or sciences programs and only one-fourth in professional curricula;[25] and this concentration, together with other factors, has created massive unemployment or underemployment, not conducive to widespread expansion of external degrees of the sort found in Britain.

The University of London also served as a model for an institution now known as the University of South Africa. The University of the Cape of Good Hope was founded in 1873 and two years later received from Queen Victoria a royal charter granting it the right to confer degrees which, as the current *University Calendar* notes, "are entitled to the same rank, precedence, and consideration as the degrees of any university in the United Kingdom." These degrees were awarded on the basis of study undertaken at any of the eight colleges of South Africa. In 1916, the country's university system was reconstructed, the name of the governing institution was changed to the University of South Africa, the universities at Stellenbosch and Capetown were given the independent right to award degrees, and the other six (plus a later institution) continued under the authority of the newly named university. Six of the seven began a process of growth, and by 1951 all had achieved independence; one declined and eventually died.

In 1946, the University began a new function which has since become its dominant service. Just as the University of London finally initiated instruction in 1900, so the University of South Africa began it forty-six years later. In the latter case, however, instruction was provided not in classrooms but by correspondence study. A student who wishes to enroll must first meet the matriculation requirements which follow South African practices and use

[25] P. G. Altbach, "Higher Education in India," in B. B. Burn and others, *Higher Education in Nine Countries* (New York: McGraw-Hill, 1971), p. 332.

procedures and nomenclature too complex for explanation here. Presumably they are about the equivalent of those required for entry into any other South African university. After admission, the student pursues his study in one or more of thirty-six fields organized into courses taught by faculty members having equal status with professors at other universities in the country. The degrees offered are: the baccalaureate, the honours baccalaureate, the master's, and the doctorate; diplomas and certificates are awarded also, some of them postgraduate. Students may form discussion groups, they may write letters to or call upon their instructors, and during summer vacation they may attend special schools. Essentially, however, teaching is by correspondence, and learning is undertaken independently. Textbooks, supplementary readings, audiotapes, and, where necessary, other materials are sent to the student by mail. In mid-1972, there were 29,289 students directly enrolled in courses taught by 524 instructors. Examinations over the courses are offered in about five hundred centers in the country and abroad. Ashby concludes that "notwithstanding the difficulties of preparing for university degrees by correspondence, there is every reason to believe that the standard of achievement required for a degree in the University of South Africa is about the same as that required for degrees in the other universities in the Republic."[26]

In 1959, the University also accepted the responsibility for developing a group of five colleges for non-white students, created to provide a separate education for those restricted from enrolling at existing universities. Initially, the degrees for the graduates of these five colleges were awarded by the University of South Africa, but now all have achieved independent degree-granting status.

The question naturally arises as to the influence on the University of apartheid, the official government doctrine which calls for the separation of Bantus, coloureds, Asians, and whites. In 1970 the population of South Africa consisted of 15,057,952 Bantus, 2,018,-453 coloureds, 620,436 Asians, and 3,751,328 whites. Thus the total nonwhite population was 17,696,841, or 83 percent of the total.[27] On June 6, 1972, there were 39,289 students consisting of 23,339

[26] Ashby, p. 345.
[27] *State of South Africa Handbook: 1972* (Johannesburg: De Gama Publishers, 1972), p. 11.

(80 percent) whites and 5950 (20 percent) nonwhites. Of those securing degrees in April–May 1972, 869 were white and 206 were nonwhite. The recipients of diplomas and certificates were divided between 356 whites and 61 nonwhites. The academic staff, 96 percent of it full-time, included 516 whites and 8 nonwhites, the latter teaching only the Bantu languages.

Many non–South Africans are tempted to believe that the University is an instrument of apartheid because correspondence instruction is a method ideally suited to such a purpose. This impression is reinforced because the *University Calendar,* in telling students how to get supplementary books, lays heavy stress on the Nonwhite Divisions of the State Library and the Johannesburg Public Library. On the other hand, the *Calendar* also notes that "each July vacation schools, which are open to all its students, are held by the University in Pretoria." However, a letter from the University's Bureau of University Research makes clear the fact that these vacation schools are segregated: one for whites, one for Bantus, and one for Asiatics and coloureds. Of the students who attended such schools in July 1972, 3404 were white and 1268 were nonwhite. Thus it is clear that these vacation schools are organized "in accordance with the laws of the country and also in compliance with the social customs of the people." They are, in fact, "organized in those residential areas where the whites and nonwhites normally reside."[28] The conclusion is, therefore, that the vacation schools are as much reinforcers of apartheid as is the correspondence method of instruction.

Other Developments

These examples, drawn almost entirely from experience in England and countries which have followed its example, merely begin the account of the external degree as it is found throughout the world and indicate a few ways by which it has been organized. The literature on the subject (special reports,[29] national descrip-

---

[28] Data and quotations are drawn from correspondence with various officials of the University, including Professors S. Pauw and G. H. A. Steyn.

[29] A particularly valuable recent book with an excellent bibliography of primary sources is B. B. Burn, *Higher Education in Nine Countries,* cited earlier.

tions, or such generalized reference works as Volume IV of UNES-
CO's World Survey of Education) shows a great variety of practice
from country to country as educational leaders use the external degree to achieve national aspirations and to deal with special problems.

From such accounts one gains a generalized view of what
is happening in the offering of the external degree. In Australia, at
least three universities make available the baccalaureate (and one
the master's) degree by programs of external courses. In Canada,
new ventures are being proposed and tried. In Japan seven institutions offer degrees by correspondence, and a university-of-the-air
has been inaugurated, with courses by radio and eventually by television. In the USSR, correspondence instruction for degrees is accepted as a responsibility by the state, and the student is aided in
his study by being given special privileges by his employer. In India the Minister of Education has expressed his determination to
create an open university and so, with greater or lesser vehemence,
have other educational leaders around the world, though in many
cases it is not precisely clear what they mean by this term nor how
they will program the institutions they propose to create. Much of
the talk in other countries, as in the United States, is probably over-
optimistic; but the external degree (in some form or other) appears
certain to be a part of the worldwide provision of higher education.

Conclusions and Questions

Foreign experience, both traditional and emergent, suggests
that American educators must consider profoundly their own plans
and possibilities.

One central question concerning the external degree has to
do with financial support. In virtually all countries other than the
United States, higher education is supported heavily by government
subsidy, though some funds are derived from fees, endowments, and
grants from private individuals and groups. This public support
facilitates overall planning for higher education and solves the special financial problems presented by the external degree. In the
highly decentralized American system with its emphasis on feder-
alism and with a division into public and private education, new

endeavors arise from local efforts; the need is to find special methods of finance. Is the external degree likely to flourish in the United States chiefly in centralized multicampus public systems which somewhat parallel foreign programs of higher education?

Whether public funding tends to politicize higher education and whether that danger is greater for the external (as distinguished from the internal) degree are topics which research has not considered adequately yet. The anecdotal evidence presented in this chapter suggests that different situations exist, even within the same country. The history of the external degree at the University of London shows it has been deeply enmeshed in political debates and that the University has kept control over this degree only by hard and long struggles. The Open University and the CNAA are directly related to government departments and not, like the other British universities, to the University Grants Committee, composed of university scholars who do not regard themselves as civil servants, though they serve terms as members of the fund-granting Committee. Will this difference in support have any influence on the degree of self-control of OU and CNAA? The answers are not clear yet. Birkbeck College, an integral part of the University of London, appears as academically free as any institution of higher learning can be. The reader may make his own judgments about the other examples. Generally speaking, however, politicization is a potential problem as American practice evolves.

An even more analytical distinction is also significant. It is pointed out earlier that in American practice the five basic procedures are so closely linked as to seem parts of a single process. In other countries, the forms and structures developed to award external degrees ordinarily separate one or more of these procedures from the others and give it special consideration. The one exception is degree-completion as preparation for government licensure; while important differences exist on this point among both nations and professions, significant distinctions do not appear to be made between internal and external degrees so far as licensure is concerned, though law may be an exception. In other respects, however, the differences are striking:

(1) Academic degrees are awarded by institutions other than colleges and universities, such as the CNAA.

(2) An external degree program can, as at the Open University, have a completely open admissions policy, not even restricting matriculation to those who have completed secondary school.

(3) Provisions for instruction take many forms, both traditional and unorthodox. Some of the latter reach out imaginatively beyond the space and time limitations of the campus and include correspondence study, radio and television broadcasting, and the use of decentralized counseling centers. In some cases, both the methods and the materials—such as new textbooks or audio- and videotapes—can also be used by internal-degree students and by those, both youthful and adult, who want to learn for purposes other than to secure a degree.

(4) The evaluation of the student's accomplishment may be separated institutionally from the teaching which prepares for that evaluation, as has been the case at the University of London and at many Indian universities.

(5) The awarding of the degree may be separated institutionally from admission, teaching, and evaluation, as has been done by the CNAA.

Another difference between foreign and American practice deals with the range of content and level of the degree. In the United States, discussion has focused almost entirely on the A.A., the baccalaureate, and the master's degree and has permitted them to be offered in a relatively small number of fields. But in other countries, external degrees are awarded in a large number of disciplines (both academic and professional) and at all levels from the subdegree, specialized diploma to the doctorate. Will American practice eventually lead this far?

Educational leaders who have worked out enduring plans for the external degree in other countries have not hesitated to question profound assumptions and to separate procedures which Americans believe essentially linked. The external degree cannot advance significantly beyond its present status in the United States unless an equal boldness is demonstrated here.

Why the External Degree?

❦❦❦❦❦❦❦❦❦❦❦❦❦❦❦❦❦❦❦❦❦❦

Americans wish to hobble down to posterity on the crutches of capital letters.

THOMAS CARLYLE

*T*he external degree exists in foreign countries almost entirely to deal with scarcity of educational opportunity; this scarcity may be general, as in England, or specific, as in Australia where segments of the population live far from a university. In the United States, on the other hand, the motivations which foster interest in the external degree (as well as in suggestions for other reforms) are mixed and complex. In part, they arise from a sense of egalitarianism; as is true abroad, a desire exists to broaden the base of opportunity, to care for segments of the population which have been underserved in the past. In part, the motivations spring from an attempt to confront the intractable problems causing the malaise and trouble apparent in American higher education today; some people believe that the sponsorship of an exter-

45

nal degree may be one way to solve these. In part, the motivations have their source in major changes in methods of instruction and in the assessment of education, making it feasible to award the external degree and, incidentally, to provide new alternatives of structure and practice so much in tune with modern times that they force changes in the cobwebbed traditions of the internal degree. Finally, motivation to provide the external degree has arisen from the manifest needs of three diverse kinds of people in modern society: the talented, those who missed a first chance at higher education and wish a second, and those who previously were not thought intellectually able to undertake college work. Chapter Three deals in depth with the major reasons for the current interest in the external degree.

Existence of a Potential Clientele

The dramatic growth of higher education in the United States since the end of World War II and, particularly, the rapid rise in the number of community colleges in the 1960s gives evidence of the desire of Americans for greater opportunities to go beyond earlier schooling to meet their learning needs and interests. In 1950, there were 1851 institutions of higher education enrolling 3,508,000 students; by 1970, 2525 institutions enrolled 7,484,000.[1] In 1972, the number of institutions had grown to 2626;[2] an audited enrollment figure for 1972 was not available at the time this book was written.

The population contains a large number of adults who were born too early to take advantage of the widespread opportunities made available to younger men and women through the expansion of facilities of higher learning. It is these adults, now caught up in the pressures and concerns of mature life, who make up the largest potential clientele for the external degree; it is to them that attention will first be paid here. It is also true that in some respects the provisions of higher education do not seem to meet the needs of all

[1] U.S. Bureau of the Census, *Statistical Abstract of the United States, 1972* (Washington, D.C., U.S. Government Printing Office, 1972), p. 128.
[2] National Center for Educational Statistics, U.S. Office of Education, *Education Directory: Higher Education, 1971–1972* (Washington, D.C.: U.S. Government Printing Office, 1972), p. xxii.

the young people seeking internal degrees. Therefore, later in this section, the dimensions of this part of the total audience will also be explored.

A note of caution should be inserted here, however, concerning the importance of distinction between a potential and an actual clientele. If an external degree is to succeed, it must be designed carefully with an awareness of many factors, beginning with a realistic assessment of local demand. It must have the support of faculty members, administrators, and policy-makers within the institution; and effective interpretation of its nature to community sectors must be provided. Programs must be begun cautiously and procedures revised in the light of experience. Where great deprivation of educational opportunity exists, rapid expansion may be possible and necessary; elsewhere, growth must be slow and cautious while a general climate of acceptance and desire for participation is created. Planners must accept the fact that for many reasons the constant expansion of educational enrollments and programs to which American educators have become accustomed will become less rapid and may even be replaced by contraction. If the external degree is to have a viable future, it cannot be brought into being merely by opening the doors of the university at a new place or time. In many cases a potential clientele exists—but it may be neither easily discovered nor quickly served.

Adult clientele. An adult is here defined as a person who has achieved full physical development and who has assumed his right to participate as a responsible home-maker, worker, and member of society; the performance of these roles is his major preoccupation. Some people achieve this social maturity very early in life; others never accomplish it. Since, for statistical analysis, some arbitrary figure must be chosen, the age of twenty-five is here employed as a conservative dividing-point since, by this age, the responsibilities of maturity have been assumed and the period of full-time college or university attendance has ended for most.

The 1971 estimates of years of school completed by persons twenty-five years old or over with at least some high school education are presented in Table 3 (numbers of people) and in Table 4 (percentages of the total group). These tables taken together reveal

Table 3

YEARS OF SCHOOL COMPLETED BY PERSONS TWENTY-FIVE YEARS OLD AND OVER, MARCH 1971

(Numbers in thousands)

	Some High School	High School Completion	Years of College				
			1	2	3	4	5 or more
Total	18,601	38,029	4,360	5,433	1,989	7,666	4,946
All males	8,264	16,008	2,085	2,712	1,001	4,212	3,441
All females	10,339	22,021	2,276	2,721	987	3,454	1,505
Total white	16,061	35,181	4,069	5,111	1,879	7,240	4,677
White males	7,203	14,754	1,960	2,551	954	4,006	3,291
White females	8,857	20,427	2,109	2,560	926	3,234	1,385
Total nonwhite	2,541	2,848	291	322	109	426	270
Nonwhite males	1,060	1,254	125	161	48	206	150
Nonwhite females	1,481	1,594	167	161	61	220	119

NOTE: Some totals influenced by rounding.
SOURCE: U.S. Bureau of the Census, *Population Characteristics: Educational Attainment, March 1971*, Series P–20, No. 229, December 1971 (Washington, D.C.: U.S. Government Printing Office, 1971).

Table 4

Years of School Completed by Persons Twenty-Five Years Old and Over, March 1971

(by percentages)

	Some High School	High School Completion	Years of College				
			1	2	3	4	5 or more
Total	16.8	34.4	3.9	4.9	1.8	6.9	4.5
All males	15.8	30.6	4.0	5.2	1.9	8.0	6.6
All females	17.7	37.8	3.9	4.7	1.7	5.9	2.6
Total white	16.2	35.5	4.1	5.2	1.9	7.3	4.7
White males	15.3	31.3	4.2	5.4	2.0	8.5	7.0
White females	17.0	39.2	4.0	4.9	1.8	6.2	2.7
Total nonwhite	22.3	24.9	2.6	2.8	1.0	3.7	2.4
Nonwhite males	20.1	23.8	2.4	3.1	0.9	3.9	2.9
Nonwhite females	24.1	25.9	2.7	2.6	1.0	3.6	1.9

NOTE: Percentages are rounded.
Source: U.S. Bureau of the Census, *Population Characteristics: Educational Attainment, March 1971*, Series P–20, No. 229, December 1971 (Washington, D.C.: U.S. Government Printing Office, 1971.

some important facts about the level of education of American adults which will be briefly noted here.[3]

(1) The need for completion of a program is pronounced. For every subgroup defined by sex and race, the number of people finishing high school is greater than the total of those who finished all three of the previous years. In every case but one (non-white females), the number of people with two years of college is greater than the number of those who completed only one year, a fact which probably reflects the desire to complete a community college program. The holding power of the baccalaureate is also evident; the number of those who attend four years of college is in every case much higher than the number who attend only three.

(2) The differences between males and females of years of attainment reverse direction between high school and college. Many more girls than boys complete high school. In the first year of college, however, a change occurs in the percentages; more males than females attend. As the years of college progress, the differences between the sexes become more pronounced, almost always in favor of the males. In the white population the disparity is greater than in the nonwhite population.

(3) In years of school completed, whites markedly exceed nonwhites. This difference is pronounced so far as high school completion is concerned and continues to be true for both sexes in each succeeding year of education.

(4) If we assume that all high school graduates should go to college and that all persons entering college should complete a baccalaureate degree, the unserved adult potential in 1971 would have been 49,811,000. Only the most academic Utopian would ever grant these two assumptions, but this figure is mentioned here to indicate the largest present adult audience for an external baccalaureate degree. Realistic potentials are far smaller and to them we now turn.

Perhaps the individual most likely to seek an external degree

---

[3] These interpretations like later ones are stated only at the very general level required to make the points considered here. Much more subtle analyses of college attendance and completion have been made by, for example, S. B. Withey and others, *A Degree and What Else?* (New York, McGraw-Hill, 1971).

is the adult who, at some time in the past, attended college. Such a person chose to proceed with higher education, went through time-consuming and sometimes arduous admission and induction procedures, and began a program of studies which he never completed. The initial requirements—motivation and potential ability—were met, but the promise they offered was not fulfilled.

As Table 3 shows, it was estimated in 1971 that 11,782,000 adults twenty-five years of age and over had matriculated but had not gone beyond the third year of college. Of this number, those who had one year (4,360,000) or three years (1,989,000) of college, a total of 6,349,000, can be counted with some certainty as not having completed an intended degree. Of those completing two years of schooling, an unknown number were awarded their A.A. degrees and might or might not have been interested in securing a more advanced degree. In 1968, about 28 percent of the community college students in six "pacesetter" states were vocational as distinguished from transfer students.[4] This figure, however, cannot be accepted as a basis for estimating the percentage of persons not wishing to go on to the baccalaureate of the 5,433,000 people twenty-five years of age and over who had completed two years of schooling, as this percentage has not been demonstrated as either universally true or stable over a long period of time. Furthermore, the majority of students completing two years were probably in four-year colleges and universities where they were pursuing baccalaureates. Since there is no accurate way of deducting the A.A. receivers from other two-year students and since some holders of the A.A. might be interested in a baccalaureate degree were it available to them, the safest course is to identify the total group of 11,782,000 partial college attenders as potential students for the external degree.

Among people twenty-two to twenty-four years of age in 1971, the number and percentage of partial college attenders was significantly higher than the number among adults twenty-five years of age or over. In fact, as Table 5 shows, the younger age group had a higher percentage of attendance than the older one at every level of college except (understandably because of its youth) that of five years or more of study. Young men and women from twenty-

[4] L. L. Medsker and D. Tillery, *Breaking the Access Barriers* (New York: McGraw-Hill, 1971), p. 62.

Table 5

YEARS OF COLLEGE COMPLETED BY SELECTED AGE GROUPS
MARCH 1971
(by numbers and percentages)

Years of College Completed	Adults 25 Years Old and Over		Adults 22 to 24 Years of Age	
	Number[a]	Percentage of Age Group	Number[a]	Percentage of Age Group
1	4,360	3.9	784	7.7
2	5,433	4.9	819	8.0
3	1,989	1.8	631	6.2
4	7,666	6.9	1,310	12.9
5	4,946	4.5	301	3.0

[a] Numbers in thousands.
Source: U.S. Bureau of the Census, *Population Characteristics: Educational Attainment, March 1971*, Series P–20, No. 229, December 1971 (Washington, D.C.: U.S. Government Printing Office, 1971).

two to twenty-four years of age are just beyond the traditional years of college attendance; however, because of the trend toward deferred or interrupted collegiate study, many people in this age group are still full-time students unlikely to transfer to an external degree program. Even so, the 2,234,000 persons in this age group with less than four years of college probably include a sizable number of potential students for external degree programs.

Though younger adults tend to have higher rates of formal educational accomplishment than older ones, the number of people who have left college before completing four years will probably double in the next twenty years if current trends continue. Contrary to the beliefs of many people, the drop-out rate has remained fairly constant at least since the 1920s.[5] Table 6 shows certain projections

[5] J. Summerskill, "Dropouts from College," in N. Sanford (Ed.), *The American College* (New York: Wiley, 1962), p. 630; A. W. Astin, *College Dropouts: A National Profile,* American Council on Education Research Reports, Vol. 7, No. 1, February 1972.

Table 6

ESTIMATE OF PERSONS TWENTY-FIVE YEARS OLD AND OVER
COMPLETING ONE TO THREE YEARS OF COLLEGE, 1971–1990
(Numbers in thousands)

	Male	*Female*	*Total*
1971	5,798	5,984	11,782
1975	6,717	6,593	13,309
1980	8,204	7,862	16,066
1985	9,933	9,300	19,233
1990	11,622	10,683	22,305

Sources: For 1971, same as Table 1; for subsequent years, U.S. Bureau of the Census, *Current Population Reports: Demographic Projections for the United States,* Series P–25, No. 476, February 1972 (Washington, D.C.: U.S. Government Printing Office, 1972).

made by the U.S. Bureau of the Census for five-year intervals by sex for persons twenty-five years old and over. Of the two series available, the one estimating highest educational attainment is given and is therefore the more conservative estimate for present purposes. Even when one takes into account the limitations and qualifications suggested earlier (of which the most important is the growing acceptance of the A.A. as a terminal degree, whether secured internally or externally), the potential clientele for external degree programs would appear to be an enduring one for the rest of this century.

This fact has been further borne out in a national study (conducted by Alexander Astin) of college drop-outs from a representative sample of 217 institutions. All of the students concerned entered college in the fall of 1966 and four-year follow-up data were secured during the fall of 1970 and the winter of 1970–1971. Various measures of "retention" were used but the most comprehensive was that a student was counted as retained if he or she had "received the bachelor's degree, was still enrolled for work toward a degree, *or* had transcripts sent to another institution."[6] Some students never use the transcript or, if they do, drop out of institutions to which they transfer. Using even these very general criteria, only

[6] Astin, p. 4.

65.9 percent of all students who went to two-year colleges and 81.2 percent of all students who went to four-year colleges and universities were retained. Thus approximately one-third of the students at community colleges did not complete their work and approximately 20 percent of those attending four-year colleges and universities dropped out of college. These figures show why the number of partial college attenders is being constantly replenished.

Few people would argue that all secondary school graduates should continue to college. Alternative work and educational opportunities, personal choices, and the lack of motivation or ability mean that many boys and girls should follow some other way of life than education beyond high school. Yet it is equally true that a fairly large number of young people who have the potential for successful college performance and who might find degrees rewarding both for economic and personal reasons do not secure them. Some lack the motivation to attend college upon high school graduation, acquiring it later, if then. Others find that some factor beyond their control—poverty, sex, race, place of residence, ethnic background—keeps them from going to college.

Table 7 reports the results of three large studies showing the percentage of high school graduates attending two- or four-year colleges in 1957, 1961, and 1967. Assuming that these studies accurately reflect reality, they show a greatly increasing degree of college attendance for each successive group studied. They also suggest three major barriers to higher education: low academic aptitude as measured by tests, low socioeconomic status, and membership in the female sex. Only among the most favored socioeconomic and academically gifted groups has near-saturation occurred so far as college attendance is concerned. In every other group, including those usually accepted as having adequate academic and socioeconomic potential, significantly large numbers of students do not attend either a two-year or a four-year college.

Both the numbers and percentages of people twenty-five years of age and over who had completed only high school in 1971 have already been presented in Tables 3 and 4. The Bureau of the Census has projected these figures through 1990 and the data thus derived are shown in Table 8, which uses (as before) the series based on highest educational atttainment. By 1990, a total of 58,-

Table 7

High School Graduates Attending Two- or Four-Year Colleges

Ability Quarter	Socioeconomic Quarter											
	1			2			3			4		
	1957	1961	1967	1957	1961	1967	1957	1961	1967	1957	1961	1967
	Percent			Percent			Percent			Percent		
Male												
1	6	9	33	12	14	30	18	16	29	39	34	57
2	17	16	43	27	25	39	34	36	55	61	45	61
3	28	32	60	43	38	69	51	48	68	73	72	79
4	52	58	75	59	74	80	72	79	89	91	90	92
Female												
1	4	8	25	9	12	28	16	13	36	33	26	37
2	6	13	28	20	12	36	26	21	50	44	37	67
3	9	25	44	24	30	48	31	40	68	67	65	77
4	28	34	60	37	51	73	48	71	83	76	85	93

NOTE: Both the lowest ability and socioeconomic quarters are represented by the number 1, the highest by the number 4.
Source: K. P. Cross, *Beyond the Open Door* (San Francisco: Jossey-Bass, 1971), p. 7. Original studies from which data are drawn are cited in full by Cross.

Table 8

ESTIMATE OF PERSONS TWENTY-FIVE YEARS OLD AND OVER COMPLETING HIGH SCHOOL, 1971–1990

(Numbers in thousands)

	Male	Female	Total
1971	16,008	22,021	38,029
1975	18,032	24,730	42,812
1980	20,751	27,923	48,675
1985	23,428	30,983	54,411
1990	25,605	33,358	58,965

Source: Same as Table 4.

965,000 adults will have completed high school but not gone on to college. Perhaps the progress shown in Table 7 will have continued and, by 1990, all of the people who should go to college will be in attendance there. If so, the backlog of older adults who do not desire to attend will have diminished to negligible levels. It seems likely, however, that this Utopian era will not be achieved, that the drop-out rate will continue or even accentuate and that a substantial number of adults will wish to participate in an external degree program at some level.

Some percentage of those achieving a partial secondary school education will subsequently complete it and proceed beyond it to a college degree. Such people will provide an additional (and perhaps substantial) potential clientele for the external degree. The clearest evidence on that point is provided by the results of the General Educational Development test, "a battery of five comprehensive examinations in the areas of English composition, social studies, natural sciences, literature, and mathematics. The tests are designed to measure as directly as possible the major generalizations, ideas, and intellectual skills that are the outcome of four years of high school programs of instruction. Emphasis is placed on intellectual power rather than detailed content and on the ability to comprehend exactly, evaluate critically, and to think clearly in terms of concepts and ideas."[7]

Each state and territory has established its own rules for granting a high school equivalency certificate on the basis of the GED test and what score it will accept for the purpose. A study reported in 1969 indicated that, out of 1968 institutions of higher learning responding to a questionnaire, 1641 permitted the admission of non-high-school-graduate adults who used GED test scores as evidence of their ability to undertake college work. Of the remaining institutions, 169 would not admit students on this basis, and 158 had adopted no policy on the matter.[8]

The number of people taking the GED test grew from 39,-016 in 1949 to 387,733 in 1971. Since 1954 (the first year for which such figures are available), the percentage failing to meet state standards has slowly risen from about 20 percent to about 31 percent. The average person tested is twenty-eight years old and has had ten years of formal schooling. While these figures vary somewhat from state to state, they are remarkably constant and uniform despite the great growth in the size of the program.

The percentage of those taking the examination who plan further study has slowly risen from 31 percent in 1960 to 41 percent in 1971, perhaps as a result of the increasing availability of educational institutions, particularly community colleges. Great variation exists from state to state, ranging from 11 percent in Alaska and 19 percent in Virginia to 72 percent in Illinois and 74 percent in Delaware.[9]

The number taking the GED test increased about sixfold between 1960 and 1971 and will presumably continue to rise. It may be calculated, using conservative assumptions, that in 1971 about one hundred thousand adults passed the examination with the intention of undertaking further study. That intention may or may not be carried out; if it is, their study may or may not be spon-

[7] American Council on Education, *Handbook of Official GED Centers* (Washington, D.C.: American Council on Education, 1972), p. 2.

[8] American Council on Education, *Newsletter of the Commission on Accreditation of Service Experiences,* No. 32 (Washington, D.C.: American Council on Education, 1969), p. 4.

[9] Data supplied by the American Council on Education.

sored by a college or university; and the program entered may or may not be for a degree—internal or external. However, nobody should exclude this group of ambitious and energetic people as potential clients for an external degree.

Various studies (such as one reported by Tyler[10] in 1954 and another reported by Sharon[11] in 1972) show that there is no significant difference in grade-point averages between students who enter college with a GED equivalency certificate and those who are high school graduates. "The average subject," says Sharon, "was a twenty-eight-year-old male veteran who learned about the GED program in the armed services. He took the tests in order to be able to enroll in a college. He was admitted to a college with few, if any, restrictions; and despite his relatively old age, he had little or no problem in adjusting to college. His attitudes toward certain academic and social issues were more conservative than those of the general college-student population. His formal schooling consisted of the completion of tenth grade. His subsequent withdrawal from high school was because of the need to earn money. His non-traditional education consisted primarily of independent study in technical and job-related subjects. He planned to obtain a bachelor's degree and to engage in a business career."[12]

Even though most of these students receive service-connected financial aid, the cost of their education is a serious concern, causing many to attend college part-time or to drop out of school for a term or two. For many such students, an external degree would be a boon, particularly since they are already accustomed to special and non-traditional ways of securing an education. Cornelius P. Turner, director of the GED program, has observed: "It seems to me that people who wish to earn a high school equivalency certificate are very similar in their ambitions to those who will wish to earn an external degree. In fact, I suspect that many people who

[10] R. W. Tyler, *The Fact-finding Study of the Testing Program of the United States Armed Forces Institute* (Washington, D.C.: Department of Defense, 1954).

[11] A. T. Sharon, *The Non-High-School-Graduate Adult in College and His Success as Predicted by the Tests of General Educational Development* (Princeton, N.J.: Educational Testing Service, 1972).

[12] Sharon, p. 12.

have discovered through the GED tests that they are well educated, in spite of the fact that their years of formal schooling were limited, will wish to go on to the external degree program."[13]

The studies cited previously and Dr. Turner's judgment of GED students suggest that the potential clientele of high school drop-outs for external degree programs may be greater than has previously been supposed. Table 9 provides the best available, con-

Table 9

ESTIMATE OF PERSONS TWENTY-FIVE YEARS OLD AND OVER COMPLETING NO MORE THAN 1–3 YEARS OF HIGH SCHOOL, 1971–1990

(Numbers in thousands)

	Male	*Female*	*Total*
1971	8,264	10,339	18,603
1975	8,746	11,193	19,939
1980	8,938	11,965	20,903
1985	8,969	12,619	21,588
1990	8,764	13,004	21,768

Sources: Same as Table 6.

servative estimates of the numbers in this category for five-year periods until 1990. The figures do not increase rapidly, but, assuming the continuation of present conditions, a substantial number of clients for external degree programs exist among people completing one to three years of high school.

Among those adults who might find an external degree useful, many groups can be identified which have a special need for it. For the most part, they have received an extended formal education in some alternative to the traditional collegiate or university system. They have, for example, been graduated or extensively trained by the armed services; hospital schools of nursing; proprietary schools which teach either directly or by correspondence; paraprofessional

[13] Personal letter, July 17, 1972.

training systems in health, welfare, correctional, recreational, or other agencies; law enforcement programs; the civil service system; or training services maintained by business and industry. Many have been itinerant; they have moved from one community to another on assignment, seeking better jobs, or accompanying spouses or associates. Many men and women, even if they want to, cannot secure an internal degree because of cost or inconvenience; for many, however, the opportunity to secure an external degree would be deeply rewarding either personally or occupationally.

Youth clientele. The term *youth clientele* here designates those young people who, if they had the chance, would prefer an external degree to an internal one or for whom the external degree is the only feasible one. At this time, it is impossible to make any realistic estimates of the size and nature of this clientele. Some already make this choice by attending such programs as the University Without Walls, by entering university extension degree programs after leaving high school, or by participating in some alternate system of education which they consider a substitute for college. In the future, the major factors controlling youth clientele enrollments will be the attractiveness of, the flexibility of, and the degree of public acceptance accorded the external degree program.

The belief that there is a major youth clientele for the external degree rests chiefly on the assumption that this option would provide an additional opportunity for the young men and women who do not go beyond high school or who drop out after entering college. Efforts to estimate the size of this clientele have been undertaken by querying young people already in college as to whether they would have chosen an external degree had it been available and by sending out inquiries to mailing lists, but such studies are too various and fragmentary to warrant summary here.

Total clientele. The foregoing estimates of the potential clientele for the external degree cannot be taken as establishing any probable or even possible numbers. Furthermore, the data available do not deal with graduate study though, as has already been noted in Chapter One, the M.B.A. was one of the first external degrees to be offered in the United States. Data concerning the number of people who have initiated master's degrees and doctorates without completing them is too fragmentary to allow estimates of potential advanced external-degree students.

Another body of data which does bear on the question of a total potential clientele may be secured from the *demand* study described in the Preface. A national sample representing all adults age eighteen through sixty, resident at home, and not registered full-time in any educational institution was questioned concerning the nature of the programs they were undertaking or would like to undertake. When asked: "Is there anything in particular that you'd like to know more about or would like to learn how to do better?", 76.77 percent (representing an estimated 79,800,000 people) answered in the affirmative. The respondents were then asked whether they would like credit toward a degree or certificate of satisfactory completion of learning; their responses were distributed as indicated in Table 10. One must view such responses, however, with some

Table 10

CREDIT OR CERTIFICATION DESIRED BY
WOULD-BE ADULT STUDENTS, 1972

Credit or Certification Desired	Number, in millions	Percentage
None	25.9	32.48
Certificate of satisfactory completion	16.6	20.84
Credit toward high school diploma	4.0	5.07
Credit toward skill certificate or license	15.9	19.98
Credit toward two-year college degree (A.A.)	3.2	4.02
Credit toward four-year college degree (B.A.)	6.5	8.14
Credit toward advanced degree (M.A., Ph.D.)	3.9	4.83
Other credit	0.8	0.95

NOTE: Projected against the total civilian resident population of the U.S., age eighteen through sixty, excluding full-time students, of 104 million people.

skepticism. The effort to initiate and carry through a degree plan
requires will, stamina, and a degree of ability far greater than that
needed to indicate the desire to do so; in addition, no program of
study is available to many, however greatly they desire it, because
of economic or geographic situation. Yet the number of people who
wish a degree is very large; and some of those who desire only a
certificate or no credit might be challenged by further study to undertake serious and sustained learning endeavors, particularly if
external degree programs become more diversified and more widely
available than is now the case.

If systematic higher education leading to a degree is worth
having, the data presented in this chapter suggest that both individuals and society itself are much poorer, both economically and socially, than they should be, and that the deprivation falls most
heavily on the nonwhite, on women, and on those of low socioeconomic status. Furthermore, the data suggest that unless alternatives
—among them the external degree—are provided, the deprivation
of higher education will increase during the remainder of this century.

Sense of Malaise

An awareness of this vast unserved clientele was but one
element in a growing feeling during the late 1960s that American
higher education was suffering from deep troubles which showed
every sign of becoming more accentuated. Eric Ashby, one of the
most knowledgeable foreign observers of American higher education,
points out that since 1870 the figures for resident-degree enrollment,
for numbers of faculty, and for proportion of degree-credit students
to people in the eighteen- to twenty-four-year age group, if plotted
on a logarithmic scale, would all fall on a straight line. For a hundred years, he notes, enrollments doubled every fourteen to fifteen
years.[14]

American educators have become conditioned to constant
growth, reinforced in recent years by young people born in the
"baby boom" of the late 1940s. This condition will not continue

[14] E. Ashby, *Any Person, Any Study* (New York: McGraw-Hill,
1971), p. 4.

indefinitely, and more leaders are beginning to be aware that new courses must be charted without delay for American higher education. "The decade just ahead," wrote Clark Kerr in 1968, "is the most important one of those remaining in this century."[15]

The problems of higher education were brought forcefully to world attention by the so-called student revolutions which were, in fact, sometimes guided by dissident faculty members and which caused, on occasion, a surprisingly swift abandonment of academic traditions. It became apparent that colleges and universities had deep problems. The high student drop-out rate, which occurred at even the most prestigious universities, caused particular concern. Ashby contrasts the American attrition rate of 47 percent with the British rate of 13 percent and the California Institute of Technology rate of 20 percent with the Cambridge University rate of 3 percent[16] (using percentages of class members graduated with their classmates at the end of a program). Chronic budgetary crises caused such real hardships as the abandonment of projected plans for programs and institutions, the contraction or closing of colleges, and the unemployment of faculty members. A leveling-off or decline of students occurred at many colleges as a result of the rising costs of attendance; the end of selective service exemption; the difficulty of finding suitable employment, even with a college degree; and the slackening of college attendance by the unusually large number of young people born immediately after World War II. The possibility emerged of an underused faculty (many of them with life tenure contracts); the problem was enhanced by the overproduction of new doctorates. While this last development varied according to subject matter and may have been overstressed when it first was recognized, the prospect was sufficiently frightening to cause great concern in the groves of academe.

The external degree appeared to be a partial solution to these problems. If students did not like intensive and prolonged instruction, perhaps they would take part in education fitted to a more mature lifestyle, pursued at their own rate and in their own fashion,

[15] C. Kerr, "New Challenges to the College and University," in K. Gordon (Ed.), *Agenda for the Nations* (Washington, D.C.: Brookings Institution, 1968), p. 258.

[16] Ashby, *Any Person,* pp. 18–19.

using new learning and teaching techniques, and evaluated in broad and comprehensive ways. Perhaps campus budgetary crises could be eased by institutional programs which reached new clienteles. Perhaps some of the problems of student life would disappear in a new setting; for example, *in loco parentis* or parietal rules have no meaning for the external student. Perhaps external degrees could suggest non-traditional forms of academic procedure which would improve—enthusiasts said "transform"—American academic life. Perhaps the potentially underused faculty and facilities and the increasing numbers of doctorates could find employment. And, taking another tack, perhaps programs which did not call for expensive physical plants and could achieve other economies would be less costly than traditional internal degree programs.

The proposal of this one solution to so many immediate problems caused widespread discussion (much of it unfavorable) concerning the external degree. As an abstract idea, it has now been examined from almost every point of view. The descriptions of emergent programs provided in Chapter Four suggest some of the practical opportunities and difficulties which have already arisen, and the discussion of issues in Chapters Five and Six reveals both widespread hopes and doubts. But the idea of the external degree continues to gain strength. However sophisticated or naive the discussion of such a degree as a solution to the malaise of higher education may appear, at the heart of its advocacy lies the deep and perennial egalitarianism of the American ethos, rooted in the belief that the individual should have as much education as he needs or wishes to develop his potentialities. And, in that ethos, the college or university degree is the tangible manifestation that learning has taken place.

Facilitating Elements

As Chapter One suggests, the external degree did not spring into being overnight. The way was prepared for it in the United States with the creation of the elective system in the last quarter of the nineteenth century, and both the extension and adult degrees became ways of fulfilling the desire for a symbol of academic accomplishment. But the desire to find new ways of recognizing the learning potential and accomplishment of both adults and young people intensified during World War II, chiefly from a desire to aid returning veterans. When more flexible forms of the external degree were seriously proposed in 1970, many facilitating ideas and mechanisms had already been developed. This section gives a brief account of some of them, arranged in terms of the five basic procedures discussed in Chapter Two which have traditionally been associated with the degree-awarding process.

Admission. The idea of open admission is not specifically related to the external degree but, in the minds of many people, is closely associated with it, perhaps because the English Open University has laid such great stress on freedom of access—regardless of the amount or quality of a student's previous formal education. Let us consider the application of this idea in American life.

In this country the admission to college of all persons who hold a high school diploma (or its equivalent) or even of people who never finished the secondary school is a very old practice. For most of the nation's history, this group was chiefly made up of boys and, to a lesser extent, girls from rural America who had not had access to secondary schooling. For years a "preparatory department," designed to provide a remedial program for young men and women without adequate preparation for higher education, was a recognized part of many American colleges and universities. On other campuses, similar students were handled informally by special tutoring or remedial work. The chief motivation for such arrangements may have been egalitarian, but it is also true that many of the smaller and less well established colleges might otherwise not have had enough students to survive.

As secondary education spread, a high school diploma became essential for entry into most institutions of higher education; and, during the second quarter of the twentieth century, more and more colleges and universities established high standards for matriculation, using high school grade averages and aptitude-tests scores. Consequently (particularly at the difficult-access schools), the old practice of open admission fell out of favor, though it was still practiced at many institutions, particularly those relying chiefly on pub-

lic support. But in the later sixties and early seventies, this old idea
became a major issue, particularly in its implementation at the City
University of New York.[17]

Also, as noted in the discussion of the GED examination, the
idea of "high school equivalency" took firm hold, permitting those
without formal secondary education to secure a credential which
would admit them to a college degree program. Thus, an element
essential to the concept of the external degree came into existence.

Teaching. Throughout the twentieth century, as already
noted, great expansion has occurred in the number and variety of
institutions of higher learning, a growth accentuated in recent years
by the rise of the community college. This proliferation of institutions provides the indispensable base for the external degree, but
other developments more directly concerned with its advancement
should be mentioned.

The first is the growth of adult education and its success in
dealing with such difficult problems as increasing agricultural production, solving other problems of rural life, turning civilians into
effective members of the armed forces, reducing adult illiteracy,
implementing social reform, and achieving individual satisfaction.
Any estimate of the number of adults who participate in educational activities is a product of the method of analysis used, and, as
a result, wide variations exist. The unpublished study by Carp and
Peterson to which reference has already been made estimated that
32,100,000 Americans age eighteen through sixty living in their
own homes and not in full-time residence at a school or college had
taken part in some form of adult educational activity during the
year previous to the interviews.

Large sums are now being invested in adult education. No
recent statistics are available concerning the total amount of money
involved, but a study conducted in 1971–1972 showed that the federal government was then sponsoring 143 programs in 17 departments (excluding those of the Department of Defense) in which
$4,091,597,000 was being spent for extension, continuing education,

[17] The various points of view on this topic are well presented in
W. T. Furniss (Ed.), *Higher Education for Everybody?* (Washington, D.C.:
American Council on Education, 1971).

and community service programs in which institutions of higher education had some share.[18]

This growth in adult education has not been concerned chiefly with credit programs, but it has helped shape a climate in which they could flourish. More directly related is the growth of extension credit enrollments. The data reported by some 243 universities showed that, in 1969–1970, they had 2,183,372 degree credit registrations and 260,594 nondegree credit registrations in their classes, conferences, and correspondence courses.[19] These figures do not indicate the number seeking external or other degrees, but presumably a substantial number of these individuals were involved in a sequential program of study which might eventuate in a degree.

A second development in teaching has been the growth at all academic levels of part-time degree-credit enrollments, most not registered under the special auspices of an extension division but representing people who come to the campus to take one or more courses. An estimate of the number of people involved in such study for the immediate past and future is presented in Table 11. While these straightline trend projections from earlier data may not prove totally accurate, they do suggest that, as indicated in Chapter One, the number of people who attend a college or university part-time is substantial and will continue to grow.

It cannot be determined from available sources how much overlap exists between the extension registrations given earlier and the part-time enrollments in Table 11. The data in Table 12 make clear the fact, however, that the majority of part-time students tend to be well beyond the usual age of college attendance. Perhaps it should be further noted that the distinction between a full-time and a part-time student is almost always an arbitrary one based on a definition of a "normal load" of courses. Some students take no courses at all and yet manage to be, for all practical purposes, in

[18] National Advisory Council on Extension and Continuing Education, *A Question of Stewardship* (Washington, D.C.: National Advisory Council, 1972).

[19] *Programs and Registrations, 1969–1970* (Norman, Okla.: Association of University Evening Colleges, and Washington, D.C.: National University Extension Association, n.d.), p. 30.

Table 11

DEGREE-CREDIT ENROLLMENT IN ALL INSTITUTIONS
OF HIGHER EDUCATION BY ATTENDANCE STATUS:
UNITED STATES, FALL 1960–1980

Year	Total enrollment	Full-time status	Part-time status
1960	3,582,726	2,466,000	1,117,000
1965	5,526,325	3,909,987	1,616,338
1970	7,920,149	5,489,033	2,431,116
1975	10,463,000	7,036,000	3,427,000
1980	12,050,000	7,901,000	4,149,000

Source: National Center for Educational Statistics, *Projections of Educational Statistics to 1980–1981* (Washington, D.C., U.S. Government Printing Office, 1972), p. 24.

Table 12

AGE LEVELS OF ESTIMATED PART-TIME ENROLLMENTS, 1966

(Numbers in Thousands)

Age	Males	Females	Total
17	11	10	21
18–19	92	94	186
20–21	121	127	248
22–24	252	139	391
25–29	292	158	450
30–34	195	97	292
35+	84	84	168
Total	1,047	709	1,756

Source: J. K. Folger, H. S. Astin, and A. E. Bayer, *Human Resources and Higher Education* (New York: Russell Sage Foundation, 1970), pp. 384–385.

residence. Other students taking a normal load may make only one or two visits to campus during a term, getting assignments from their instructors at the start and mailing them in at the end. As every experienced faculty member, particularly at the graduate level, knows, students are remarkably ingenious at devising patterns of study which have little resemblance to the formal registration record. Perhaps the various extremes counterbalance one another, but the fact that in 1970 about two and one-half million college and university students (out of a total of almost eight million) were identified as not pursuing full-time study indicates that the normal and accepted teaching patterns of higher education have already undergone marked changes to accommodate students who could not meet the usual space and time demands.

A third major change in teaching has been the devising of new techniques and instruments. The first to have a substantial impact on part-time work toward a degree was correspondence study —used by proprietary schools, by the Federal Government, and by nonprofit institutions since the last quarter of the nineteenth century. The next major development was the appearance of audiovisual education (chiefly motion pictures, slides, and opaque projectors) in the 1920s. In succeeding years, but particularly since 1960, a great variety of systems and methods developed—radio, television, mass book production, programmed instruction, xerography, audiotapes and LP records, videotapes, microfilm and microfiche, computer-assisted instruction, and cable television. Many of these media can be used to improve instruction itself; others conquer space, time, and other limitations which have circumscribed the internal degree.[20]

Evaluation of accomplishment. A major requirement of an external degree program which modifies an internal degree (as distinguished from an external degree which departs completely from conventional patterns) is to provide some method or methods for measuring the accomplishment of learners which are directly connected to the usual standards of courses and credits or which re-

[20] For a recent review of these new techniques and their potential uses, see Carnegie Commission on Higher Education, *The Fourth Revolution* (New York: McGraw-Hill, 1972).

ceive the general acceptance as a substitute by educational authorities. Since the end of World War II, different approaches have been adopted to meet this requirement, only a few of which can be mentioned here.[21]

In general, these approaches are of three sorts: the assignment of credit equivalencies to training programs not sponsored by colleges and universities; the assessment of an individual's experience as deserving of credit; and the passing of an achievement test which measures competence in some area of content.

Of these three, the first has been worked out most fully by the Commission on Accreditation of Service Experiences (CASE), created in 1945 by the American Council on Education to evaluate military educational programs and provide collegiate registrars and other interested persons with the information necessary for granting credit for such programs. It seemed unfair that a man or woman who had been through one or more service schools (which usually lead to advanced technical competence and include many components of general education) should be considered to have learned nothing which might be used as credit toward a degree which he might have spent the war years acquiring. The Commission has issued three editions of a guide to formal service-school courses, each of which has been examined by authorities competent to make suggestions concerning the awarding of credit.

These guides have become major works of reference for the assessment of credit. For each established service educational program, the location, the length, and the objectives are provided and the content is summarized; credit recommendations follow. In many cases, it is suggested that no credit at all be given; in others, the recommendation is highly detailed, for example, "three semester hours in transportation organization and management" or "four semester hours in supply management"; some recommendations are more general in character. For the Industrial College of the Armed Forces, a ten-month program in Washington, D.C., it is noted that the instruction changed somewhat from year to year so that the recommendation for credit depends on when the student took the

[21] A fuller treatment of this topic is given by E. W. Kimmel, "Problems of Recognition," in Gould and Cross, pp. 64–94.

course. If he registered from 1954–1955 through 1962–1963, for example, it is suggested that he be given credit for "fifteen semester hours in political science, including international relations; three semester hours in business organization and management; three semester hours in speech; and nine semester hours in recent and contemporary history."[22]

Each institution of higher learning makes its own determination of whether it will accept the Commission's recommendations. In a study reported in 1969, of 1968 institutions reporting, 1097 said they would grant credit for formal service-school courses listed in the *Guide*, 407 said they would not, and 464 said they had no established policy on the matter.[23]

The assessment of the experience of an individual to determine whether it permits the granting of credit is usually handled in one of two ways. The first, experience in which a mentor guides and directs a planned field endeavor, is part of established educational practice in fields of study such as law, medicine, education, nursing, and social work. The second form, in which a student or prospective student presents a record of past accomplishment and requests either credit or advanced placement on the basis of it, has had a great deal of attention in recent years but still presents major problems, partly because unstructured life activities often cannot be squared with formal course requirements and partly because the body of organized and theoretical knowledge which serves as the basis for formal study often is not conveyed by direct experience. A man who has farmed for a year does not necessarily have a deep knowledge of soil chemistry, and residence in a city slum may not be the equivalent of a course in urban sociology. The following case at Brooklyn College, much experienced in such evaluation, will illustrate. "A woman age fifty-three, who had had fifteen years of experience as a purchasing supervisor and office manager for a large shoe manufacturing company, was interviewed by the evaluator from

[22] C. P. Turner (Ed.), *A Guide to the Evaluation of Educational Experiences in the Armed Services* (Washington, D.C.: American Council on Education, 1968), p. 350.

[23] *Newsletter of the Commission on Accreditation of Service Experiences*, No. 32 (Washington, D.C.: American Council on Education, 1969), p. 4.

the Department of Economics, but his examination of her actual knowledge did not convince him of the immediate creditability of her experience. 'Formal economic analysis,' he wrote, 'has constituted little or no part of her intellectual experience. She requires a period of reading and independent study, concentrating on those phases of business organization and operations in which her practical experience has been most limited.' "[24]

In practice a great deal of advanced standing probably is granted as faculty members or guidance officers find ways to establish equivalency by oral tests, interviews, institutional examinations, or waivers of attendance at classes. A study reported in 1961 showed that, out of 131 evening college and extension divisions, 104 had some system of permitting advanced placement. Of these, 76 allowed students to take departmental course examinations and 27 used oral tests and interviews.[25]

The most widely publicized example of credit for life experience is Brooklyn College's program.[26] Here, content evaluators from the faculty were used. A case study gives insight into the problems encountered by those who counsel and work with adult students.

The evaluator in the Department of Art interviewed a man, age forty-nine, who was then the executive vice-president of a service corporation but had had considerable experience in writing and television. He had studied painting and fine arts informally and brought to the interview numerous examples of his work in charcoal, watercolor, and oils. His duties on the job involved blueprint-reading, mechanical drawing, and plan-making. He demonstrated to the evaluator both qualitative and quantitative performance in the handling of color, drawing, and form. He also passed performance tests of his ability to do projection sections, plans,

[24] B. H. Stern, *Never Too Late for College* (Chicago: Center for the Study of Liberal Education for Adults, 1963), p. 9.

[25] *College Without Classes* (Chicago: Center for the Study of Liberal Education for Adults, 1961), pp. 5–10.

[26] The most recent work describing the total Brooklyn experience and giving citations to earlier sources is M. S. Jacobson, *Night and Day* (Metuchen, N.J.: Scarecrow Press, 1970).

and isometrics. He was examined in contrast printing, developing, enlarging, mounting, and other photographic techniques. In addition, he was examined in the history of drawing and in his knowledge of standard works of arts. As a result, credit was recommended for courses in Design, Photography, Contemporary Art, and Mechanical Drawing.

This same man had also had long experience in the business world. The evaluator from the Department of Economics studied his experience as an executive and examined him in business practice, industrial relations, managerial labor policies, market development, price control, cost, and financing. Results of this examination showed that the candidate had at least the equivalent knowledge of students who had taken courses in Introduction to Business, Labor Problems, Personnel Management, and Commodity Distribution; credit was recommended for these courses.[27]

Valuable though such systems of personal assessment may be in easing regulations and in allowing for advanced placement, the cost in time and the validity and reliability of the results are so uncertain as to lead to the belief that the method could not be used on any mass basis. Moreover, the tradition of formal examinations to measure achievement runs deep in both Eastern and Western cultures, causing doubt concerning any degree not based upon formal assessment, whether it be terminal (as in England) or intermittent (as in the United States). A major advancement of the external degree would occur if new confidence-inspiring techniques could be devised to measure the educative effect of experience.

The third method of assessing student progress is by written examinations covering either a general field of knowledge or a specific subject. Until recently, there has been no practical way to use this method of validation for an external degree in this country. Contacts between the American and the English academic community have been long and close; the University of London external degree has been well known on this side of the Atlantic for many years. From time to time, American educators have studied that

[27] Stern, p. 8.

degree, and some have proposed that it be adopted in this country. But the United States had no fitting evaluative mechanism; the intermittent and localized methods of assessment customary in this country could not be as readily adapted to the external degree as could the English pattern of culminative and centralized evaluation.

The creation and validation of college-level achievement examinations began to fill this gap in the 1960s and early 1970s.[28] The effort to build a system of assessment which would measure American practice and thereby provide the missing element in programs for the external degree has a short but complex history, as yet unwritten. Perhaps behind all the ventures was the success of the GED program at the secondary school level and the realization that something similar should be possible in higher education. Also, the Advanced Placement Program of the College Entrance Examination Board undoubtedly had an influence on the growth of content examinations for higher education. This program offers college-level courses in high schools. Students who pass such courses—on the basis of examinations constructed and graded by the Educational Testing Service (ETS) with the assistance of secondary school and college faculty members—are given credit or advanced standing when they enter college. This program began in the early 1950s and has flourished since. In May 1972, for example, 58,828 candidates from 3397 schools took 75,199 examinations.[29]

An early effort to use course examinations to measure adult achievement was made by the New York State Education Department in 1963 when it created the College Proficiency Examination Program (CPEP) which made available to the residents of that state course-oriented tests developed by faculty members of New York institutions of higher learning. Another effort was examined by the Committee on Institutional Cooperation, a consortium of leading midwestern universities. Limited ventures were undertaken in various places, and the number of institutions and associations interested in a generalized examination program constantly grew.

[28] In the archives of ETS is a memorandum by Robert J. Solomon dated March 13, 1959, which proposes "the development of a comprehensive battery of tests of liberal arts college achievement" and identifies the essential nature of the program planned.

[29] Information supplied by Jane Sehmann of ETS.

Meanwhile, in the early 1960s, the Educational Testing Service had started to experiment with measures of college-level achievement which were then known as Comprehensive College Tests. By 1965, these tests had been sufficiently well developed for general use. Such tests, it was thought, could achieve a number of purposes, as defined by the 1966–1967 Annual Report of ETS: "evaluate the status of those whose education has not followed the typical pattern, establish standards for award of college credit for work done under patterns different from traditional college instruction, assist in the guidance and selection of students for upper-level study, and help colleges assess the effectiveness of their curricula."[30]

Many efforts were consolidated in 1965 when the College Entrance Examination Board, after discussions with ETS and a thorough review of the issues, became the sponsor of the Comprehensive College Tests by creating a council of educators who could accept responsibility for what came to be called the College-Level Examination Program (CLEP).[31] The Carnegie Corporation provided a grant to support further development. (By 1973, it had made three grants for CLEP totaling $3,100,000.)

The CLEP examinations are of two sorts. One is made up of general examinations in English composition, the humanities, the natural sciences, mathematics, and the social sciences including history. The other is made up of subject examinations in such content areas as educational psychology, English composition, geology, introductory sociology, and statistics. Examinations are given at test centers administered by ETS, at colleges, and to service personnel through the auspices of the United States Armed Forces Institute.

The CLEP examinations have a number of uses not contemplated in earlier days, among them the selection of undergraduate students for special honors programs and the evaluation and placement of foreign students. From a rather slow beginning, the

[30] *Annual Report, 1966–1967* (Princeton, N.J.: Educational Testing Service, 1968), pp. 41–42.

[31] Anyone wishing to examine the early history of the tests will find two documents particularly useful. One is J. N. Arbolino, *The Council on College-Level Examinations* (New York: College Entrance Examination Board, 1965) and the other is R. L. Flaugher, M. H. Mahoney, and R. B. Messing, *Credit by Examination for College-Level Studies: An Annotated Bibliography* (New York: College Entrance Examination Board, 1967).

number of people involved has risen dramatically; in 1971–1972, a total of 108,400 candidates took 371,500 tests. Many who wish to secure credit by examination do so by taking the tests at the CLEP test centers. In 1967–1968, when the program was begun, 1464 candidates took tests at these centers; in 1971–1972, the number had risen to 21,393 taking 73,559 general examinations and 6570 subject examinations. About half the examinations at ETS centers are taken by people age twenty or less, but the age range of the other candidates is broad. For example, in 1971–1972, people age fifty or older took 631 general examinations and 139 subject examinations.

Meanwhile, the number of colleges and universities agreeing to use CLEP in some way has steadily risen and, in mid-1972, included more than 1100 institutions. Various studies have been conducted on the performance of people taking the examinations. The largest was an analysis of the scores of 43,877 military personnel in which it was shown that "depending on the test, from 12 to 27 percent of the servicemen who have not studied beyond the high school level scored as well as the average college sophomore."[32]

As yet, those considering the role of CPEP, CLEP, or other written examinations in external degree programs have treated them as partial measures of accomplishment—to be used along with course grades, credit equivalents, and assessments of work experience in fulfilling the total requirements of a degree pattern. The awarding of a degree solely on the basis of examinations, a familiar practice in England for a century and a half, has not yet been introduced on a widespread and general scale in this country, though, as Chapter Four will show, it is now being undertaken. It is likely that the development of college-level achievement testing (particularly the breadth and national coverage of CLEP) will prove to have been the most significant factor in laying the groundwork for the external degree in the United States.

Certification. The issuance of a degree or certificate implies that the issuing institution has established its right to do so, usually by some fairly rigorous process of accreditation. In most

[32] A. T. Sharon, "Adult Academic Achievement in Relation to Formal Education and Age." *Adult Education,* 1971, *21*:4, 231.

countries, this right is conferred by government, usually by the granting of a charter. In the United States, however, many different practices and policies exist. Education is a function of the state, rather than the national, government; therefore, policies of accreditation and the vigor with which standards are enforced vary not only from state to state but also from one administration to another. But the major task of certifying the quality of institutions is private, not public, and is a process of both stimulation and policing. Traditionally regional accrediting associations have exercised the greatest sanctions as guarantors of standards and will doubtless continue to do so (paricularly as they draw closer together nationally). Meanwhile the accreditation of training programs for the various professions is carried out by associations within each profession.

The diversity of accrediting authorities is complicated by the variety of institutions and programs. In the United States, the reliance on institutional or system autonomy has been conducive to a much more open and varied approach to the awarding of degrees than is the case in countries where the number and kinds of institutions are rigidly controlled by centralized authorities. Different sets of standards are required; for example, the community college, the four-year liberal arts college, the separate technical school, and the comprehensive graduate university all cannot be judged by the same accreditation policies and procedures. The programs offered also vary greatly. As noted in Chapter One, more than 1600 different American degrees existed by 1960, and there are many more now. Each institution should meet the standards which qualify it to award every degree it offers. And the American higher education system is so massive that the establishment and maintenance of quality throughout its whole imposes vast problems.

The growth of the external degree and other forms of nontraditional study has complicated the situation, since it requires a profound reconsideration of the theory and practice of accreditation. In general, the right to award a particular degree has been based on whether the sponsoring institution has the resources and follows the practices which experienced educators believe necessary. But, as proponents of other points of view have vehemently asserted, at least two other tests could be applied. One is an estimate of the product of the system: Does the person certified for the degree ac-

tually have the knowledge, skill, and sensitiveness which possession
of the degree implies? Another test (one which community-college
leaders feel to be particularly appropriate) rests on what economists call a "value-added" concept. How effectively in terms of its
stated aims has a degree program influenced the students whom it
accepted? Those who consider this question crucial articulately express the belief that "high-prestige" institutions (which often feel
themselves above any need for accreditation) act merely as con-
duits, choosing only the ablest students, those unlikely to fail in any
situation, and moving them along a smooth passage from entry to
exit, hardly influencing them at all.

The vigorous presentation of such nonconformist points of
view, striking at the heart of the accreditation process, has had an
influence on the credential-establishing apparatus in the United
States, particularly because the sharp questions about policy come
at the time of general malaise in higher education. Various specific
issues will be raised later, but in general the national and regional
accrediting authorities have been cautiously receptive to the idea
of the external degree, sometimes taking the initiative either in ad-
vancing it or providing forums for discussion.

This open-mindedness has required a certain amount of
courage because many of the arguments for non-traditional education are readily adopted by charlatans who hope to turn a profit by
awarding degrees which require little or no effort or by well-intentioned but ineffectual founders of institutions which do not have
the resources to select students carefully, to educate them effectively, or to evaluate their learning properly. The diploma mill has
long been a common phenomenon in American life, as has the existence of well-intentioned but fatuous sponsors of visionary schemes.
Whatever basis for accreditative judgment is used, hard practical
scrutiny exercised over a period of time by objective observers is required to certify that an institution has the right to award degrees.
The long-range test of whether the external degree should be a permanent part of American higher education is likely to come from
the effectiveness with which it establishes the right to certify its
students.

This is probably the reason why most attention has been
devoted to the external awarding of the associate degree and the

baccalaureate. As yet, the first of these has no deep traditions, since it was created to meet modern needs and conditions and therefore lent itself unusually well to varied patterns of part-time and independent study. The extension and adult degrees have been chiefly at the baccalaureate level, and the assessment degree has followed these precedents. As yet, few significant changes have been made by established accredited institutions to allow for external study in either the advanced professional degree (with the exception of the M.B.A.) or the Ph.D. Some special programs at these levels have been created at new colleges and universities but they have not yet achieved independent recognition. In Britain and other countries which award the advanced external degree, internal programs of preparation are less formally structured than in the United States (which is often accused of "spoon-feeding" its graduate and professional students); and this fact, perhaps, has led to the fairly extensive provision for advanced external degrees in such countries.

Licensure. Licensure is not essentially a part of the academic process, since it is the awarding—usually by the state—of the right to practice a specific profession. The relationship of licensure to colleges and universities is that graduation from an approved program of studies may be a requirement, but practices vary greatly from profession to profession and from state to state. In some highly skilled occupations, such as farm operation or business management, no license is required. The conflict between the "university" law school and the "night" law school has been long and bitter. The same license to practice nursing is awarded to graduates of two-year community college programs, three-year diploma programs, and four-year baccalaureate programs. While several recent major studies have examined licensing practices, particularly within the health professions, practice so far as licensure is concerned is far from stable.

As yet, no major changes in licensure have occurred to facilitate the growth of the external degree. Most such degrees have been in the liberal or general studies or in occupations which do not require licensure (such as business management) or they have been so designed as not to violate existing requirements. In the long run, the growth of new degrees may be hampered by licensing restrictions, and academic leaders may need to exert their influence to change the legislative or administrative regulations which limit the practice of an occupation to those who have internal degrees. Such changes may not be difficult, since academic leaders are often members of state licensing authorities or key advisors to them.

New Alternatives

The development of each of the four major academic elements in the degree-awarding process (admission, teaching, assessment, and certification) during the 1960s made it possible to serve new clienteles or to cure some aspects of the malaise of colleges and universities. Chapter Four provides an account of how some institutions went about this task, but a retrospective view of the data presented in Chapter Three suggests that, consciously or unconsciously, university policy-makers and administrators identify at least three major groups of students as target audiences at which external degree programs might be aimed.

The first, and perhaps the largest, group of potential students for the external degree are people who have traditionally been considered "good college material" but who, for one reason or another, lacked the opportunity to attend or did not take advantage of that opportunity. The data in the various tables in this chapter show that many academically capable men and women (particularly the latter) have either not gone to college or have not completed their programs once there, and that straight-line extrapolations of current trends indicate that the number of such people will rise, not decline, during the rest of this century.

It is sometimes argued that the current situation balances out many known and unknown factors so that at least a rough kind of justice is done and the people with the capacity to secure degrees are, in fact, receiving them. In a section entitled "The So-called Pool of Ability," the Robbins Committee of Great Britain pays its respects to this point of view:

> *We believe that it is highly misleading to suppose that one can determine an upper limit to the number of people who could benefit from higher education, given favourable circumstances. It is, of course, unquestionable that*

human beings vary considerably in native capacity for all sorts of tasks. No one who has taught young people will be disposed to urge that it is only the difference in educational opportunity that makes the difference between a Newton or a Leonardo and Poor Tom the Fool. But while it would be wrong to deny fundamental differences of nature, it is equally wrong to deny that performance in examinations or tests—or indeed any measurable ability—is affected by nurture in the widest sense of the word . . . It is no doubt true that there are born a number of potential 'firsts' whose qualities are such that they win through whatever their environmental disadvantages, and another, considerably larger, number who, if trained by the most famous teachers in history, would still fail their examinations. But in between there is a vast mass whose performance, both at the entry to higher education and beyond, depends greatly on how they have lived and been taught beforehand.[33]

The committee goes on to cite studies showing that "fears that expansion would lead to a lowering of the average ability of students in higher education have proved unfounded."[34]

Studies in the United States have produced the same results. John Folger, Helen Astin, and Alan Bayer introduce a review of such studies by saying that "some educators have argued that, with the increased proportions of high school students now attending college, the ability level of entering freshmen must inevitably drop and many higher educational institutions become less selective. So far, however, their dire predictions seem to have no basis in fact."[35] Essentially the same conclusion was reached by Paul Taubman and Terence Wales who, using economic techniques to analyze the changes from the mid-1920s to the mid-1960s, discovered that "it is apparent that the quality of college students has not declined. In fact, throughout this period of forty years, during which a substantially greater percentage of high school graduates entered college, it

[33] *Higher Education,* pp. 49–50.
[34] *Higher Education,* p. 53.
[35] J. K. Folger, H. S. Astin, and A. E. Bayer, *Human Resources and Higher Education* (New York: Russell Sage Foundation, 1970), p. 158.

has even noticeably increased." The chief reason offered for their conclusion is that "in the 1920s only about 60 percent of the most able high school graduates entered college, whereas by the 1960s the corresponding figure was about 90 percent."[36]

Such studies suggest (though they certainly do not prove) that an external degree program might well be useful in reaching some of those adults who demonstrate their ability in high school but who do not go to college or who enter college but do not complete degree programs. As the figures presented earlier in this chapter abundantly attest, a large potential market for the external degree exists among the same kinds of people whom colleges have always served, particularly those denied access to colleges by circumstances beyond their control.

If the external degree were proposed only as a substitute for the internal degree and were intended chiefly for young people of college age, serious questions could be raised as to whether some subtle discrimination were not being practiced. Elias Blake has made this point with some force:

> *Large numbers of minority groups are just now approaching what they know to be a way towards upward mobility inside the American system. And just at the point when they are making their great big move, the system all of a sudden begins to change in radical ways. Well, we in the minority group community are very paranoid about that sort of thing. We wonder when things begin to change just when we begin to reach for the ring and the ring is somewhere else and it's a new ring of which no one is very certain about the shape. We don't really know what grip to put on it, how high to reach for it, or how fast you have to run to grab hold of it. We say, at this point of bewilderment, "Couldn't you just let enough parts of the present system stay where it is until we get our numbers up; until we begin to get our flow out of it?" I think there will be some suspicion generated about the external degree pro-*

[36] P. Taubman and T. Wales, *Mental Ability and Higher Educational Attainment in the 20th Century,* Occasional Paper 118 (Washington, D.C.: National Bureau of Economic Research, 1972), p. 19.

*grams, for example, or the open university kind of program
where there really is no campus or coming together. It will
be a while before higher education itself readjusts these
kinds of notions, and I repeat, there will be a great deal of
suspicion about whether these changes will serve the real
interests of getting larger numbers of minority group students into and through these institutions.*[37]

Some of the sting of Blake's comment is removed when the
external degree is designed chiefly for adults, where it may be able
to provide a genuine and important service for both minority groups
and others who have been denied college education earlier. The
record of the GED examination suggests that, as an alternate route
to a high school diploma equivalency, it has provided a valuable
second chance to those who missed their first one. Perhaps the external degree, when fully developed, can have the same effect.

A second target audience for the designer of an external degree is made up of people of unusually high ability. Such students
might fairly be called elite, but it would be a meritocratic elite,
made up either of people who had somehow missed their opportunity earlier or who had developed their ability after leaving
school.

Ashby has put very well the case for the nurturance of this
group:

*All civilized countries . . . depend upon a thin
clear stream of excellence to provide new ideas, new techniques, and the statesmanlike treatment of complex social
and political problems. Without the renewal of this excellence, a nation can drop to mediocrity in a generation. The
renewal of excellence is expensive: the highly gifted student
needs informal instruction, intimate contact with other first-
class minds, opportunities to learn the discipline of dissent
from men who have themselves changed patterns of thought
. . . De Tocqueville long ago predicted that [the nurtur-*

[37] "Commentary," *Association of Governing Boards of Universities
and Colleges Reports*, 1971, *14*(3), 15–16.

ance of such an elite] *would be anathema in an egalitarian society. He was right: by a curious twist of reasoning, persons who enthusiastically agree to supernormal educational expenditure on the intellectually underprivileged, oppose supernormal expenditure on the intellectually overprivileged, who need it just as much.*[38]

The figures summarized in Table 7 show that a substantial percent of high school graduates in the top quarter of ability are not going to college. Astin's study of drop-outs discovered that of the students securing A or A+ averages in high school, only 93 percent were retained in four-year colleges and universities and 88 percent were retained in two-year colleges. For students with an A— average, the comparable figures were 90 percent and 78 percent.[39] These studies make clear the fact that even of the people who demonstrate very high promise early in life, significant numbers do not go on to college or, if they do, do not complete their stay. More than that, the promise and the motivation of many gifted people are not evident in youth. It is often true, for example, that senior admirals and generals turn out to be men who did not rank near the top of their classes at the service academies; the armed services have made provision for that fact by designing a lifetime career of education to develop latent talents. Some such programs of external study might prove highly rewarding to civilian society as well—and at least some of them should be so devised as to award degrees.

Some external degree programs have, in fact, already been designed to reach unusually capable people, particularly of two sorts: women and business executives. In the first case, formal study may have been denied because of poverty, race, place of residence, or because a family chose to send a son to college rather than a daughter. The completion of college may have proved impossible, either for economic reasons or because marriage or some other way of life exerted a more powerful appeal. In the second case, the tests and challenges of commercial life may have caused a young man to demonstrate a previously undiscovered flair for accomplishment.

[38] Ashby, *Any Person,* pp. 101–102.
[39] Astin, pp. 20, 22.

In both cases the standards of achievement in the external degree programs are set very high. Some of the programs for unusually competent women have shown tolerance for men and perhaps may eventually become bisexual.

A third target audience is those people who fall below the customary standards of college admission but who still want to secure a college education. As open admission has been adopted by formerly limited-access institutions and as community colleges have proliferated, the group of new students who have been attracted has been intensively studied, most fully and directly perhaps by K. P. Cross in *Beyond the Open Door*. Such studies show that if these people (whom Cross defines as "scoring in the lowest third among national samples of young people on traditional tests of academic ability") are to secure degrees, educators must emphasize not openness of access to college nor remedial programs which fit students into standardized patterns but rather a clear definition of the goal to be reached. Cross puts the point succinctly: "The newest form of certification—the external degree—is the exact opposite of the present certification. Advocates of the external degree propose to certify the level of accomplishment regardless of the pathways used to reach it—a quite different concept from that used in certifying the pathways regardless of the final level of accomplishment."[40]

External degree programs for these new students, whether of customary college age or adult, must be designed with special attention to both teaching and assessment. Such people are ordinarily not gifted in independent, print-oriented learning; they need the stimulation of a mentor or a group of like-minded people who will challenge them but not overassist them. Often they need counseling of both an academic and an emotional sort, the latter including in its purposes the reinforcement of their self-esteem. As for evaluation, some use may be made of pencil-and-paper tests based on established fields of content, but new kinds of testing mechanisms are also required which will measure the learning outcomes of life experience which can be related to the pattern of objectives of the degree itself.

In concluding both this section and this chapter, however,

[40] Cross, p. 164.

it may be well to say yet again that while educators propose, students dispose. A very large number of people who might be attracted to an external degree program if it were well planned and constructed clearly exists. Such people, who are not spread uniformly throughout the country, can be at least roughly separated into categories which provide useful, indeed essential, beginning-points for the designing of programs. However, once a program gets under way, it will develop a life and clientele of its own. And in that emerging clientele, new and sometimes surprising clusters of people will emerge from both the adult and the youth clienteles who find that the external degree helps them meet their need for an organized and meaningful comprehensive learning program.

The Current
Scene

❧❧❧❧❧❧❧❧❧❧❧❧❧❧❦❦❦❦❦❦❦❦❦❦❦❦❦❦

The scene is a changing scene because it is alive.

RED SMITH

*E*xternal degrees, like computers, come in "generations," in each of which some new theory, organizing principle, or invention creates an advance in potential service. In the United States, the first generation was the extension degree, the second was the special degree for adults, and the third is here called the assessment degree. Each of the first two has many different forms and patterns; so does the third. As with computers, examples of the older generations continue to be used by those who have grown accustomed to them or who are unable, for one reason or another, to shift to a new way of work. But the third generation has attracted enough attention and a sufficiently large group of supporters that, while its essence is hard to define, it has clearly made its presence felt.

In this chapter, some estimates of the scope of the three generations of the external degree will be given, but primary attention

87

will be devoted to the third. The main body of the chapter some-what paralleling Chapter Two, provides brief accounts of several programs to show the diversity of thought of the planners rather than the extent to which they have realized their plans. Desirable as the latter would be, the growth and evolution of programs is so swift that a status report presented on any one day would be obso-lete on the next.

Extension Degree

The extension degree, in its purest form, is one awarded on completion of a coherent and complete traditional degree program offering all necessary subjects and options at a time or place accessi-ble to those who cannot come to the campus or whose other respon-sibilities make it necessary for them to spread their study over a longer period than does the student on campus. In admission, in-struction, evaluation, and certification, few or no changes are made. As the director of one such program observed, "we serve the old wine in old bottles, but we do so in a new location and we dole it out over a longer period of time."

Countless adaptations which change or modify the form of the extension degree exist, but they do not destroy its essence. Inter-nal students may be admitted to some or all extension classes, and extension students may take some of their work at internal classes or at other educational institutions. Sometimes, as at Harvard which offers both the B.A. and the A.A. in extension, courses are taught by television or in other non-traditional ways. At some institutions, the part-time internal student may develop a program hard to dif-ferentiate from that of the part-time extension student. Special ad-mission requirements may be established for some or all students, and transfers from other institutions may be handled on special bases. Departments of study may make varying regulations, refrain entirely from the degree program, or establish their own extension-degree sequences. In large, complex universities, the requirements may differ radically from one school to another. Thus, a school of business may offer one or more complete extension degree pro-grams, while all other departments of instruction are restricted by institutional bylaws from doing so or are allowed to provide some courses externally but not to build a complete degree sequence. Complicated fee structures may be devised. All this diversity leads on many campuses to a nightmarish set of regulations and requirements obscured by a cloud of exceptions and special provisions created by precedent, privilege, and negotiation.

However hard to administer such a set of policies and exceptions may be, it is often defended on the basis of the need for flexibility and of a desire to meet the varying situations which occur as the university comes into contact with the community. The effort to reduce the national offering to a coherent pattern more specific than that suggested by Carey (described in Chapter One) may well be doomed to failure. Anyone who wishes to examine this diversity at first hand, however, may do so by reviewing the results of the data-collection efforts of the Association of University Evening Colleges (AUEC). The most recent and comprehensive report of this organization describes the work at 146 institutions. While this is a far-from-complete listing of institutions which offer the extension degree, it provides abundant evidence of the complexity of the programs available.[1]

Adult Degree

The adult degree, in its purest form, was developed in the belief that adults, both psychologically and socially, are so distinctively different from young people that a program of studies designed for men and women should be based at every point on their maturity. Such a degree may depart completely from traditional patterns of admission, instruction, evaluation, or certification, or it may mix new elements with old ones so that some compatibility exists between it and an extension or an internal degree. In either case, however, the guiding principle is that the students are men and women, not late-adolescents. Old wine may or may not be used, but it is served from new decanters.

After a rather slow start in the 1950s and 1960s, interest in the adult degree picked up rapidly. In a 1969 study reported by the

[1] W. A. Hoppe (Ed.), *Policies and Practices in Evening Colleges 1971* (Metuchen, N.J.: Scarecrow Press, 1972).

AUEC, 104 institutions responded to the question "Do you offer a special degree program for adults?" Of these, 24 (23 percent) said yes. Of the 98 institutions who answered the question "Are you considering offering a special degree program for adults in the near future?", 28 (29 percent) said yes.[2] In a replication of the study two years later, 110 institutions answered the first question, 40 (36 percent) saying yes, and 98 answered the second question, 38 (39 percent) saying yes.[3]

Because no clear definition is given of the term *special degree program for adults,* one cannot be sure that all respondents had adult degrees in mind and were not referring only to some adaptation of a conventional extension degree. The list of institutions responding (since it was drawn largely from the membership of the AUEC which has a central concern with external degrees) is not broadly representative of American higher education, though examples of every sector are included. Despite these qualifications, however, it is probably significant that the percentages increase substantially in a two-year period. In 1969, half of the institutions were either sponsoring special degree programs for adults or were contemplating doing so. Only two years later, three-fourths were in one or the other category.

Assessment Degree

The third-generation external degree, emphasizing assessment and demonstration of competence, is developing on the basis that one or more of the traditional procedures of higher education—admission, teaching, evaluation, certification, or licensure—can be so modified or separated from the others that the actual learning of the student, rather than his completion of formal requirements, can become the center of attention and the basis of the awarding of the degree. Since most students in an assessment degree program are adults, its nature and form may seem to overlap that of the adult degree. The essential idea of each, however, is readily distinguishable, not only because the assessment degree is projected

[2] W. A. Hoppe (Ed.) *Policies and Practices in Evening Colleges 1969* (Metuchen, N.J.: Scarecrow Press, 1969), pp. 25, 27.
[3] Hoppe (1971), pp. 37, 53.

as a way to serve young people as well as adults, but because it so clearly emphasizes certification of competence.

Sometimes it is hard to draw the line which distinguishes some simple change in procedure from an alteration of fundamental requirements. As Paul Dressel has remarked, "much of what passes as innovation in colleges and universities is really only faddism and tinkering. Changes in requirements, changes in grading practices, freshman seminars, independent study, or alternatives in the calendar are often introduced into or grafted onto a program without really modifying the views or the instructional practices of the faculty."[4] Those who advocated the second-generation external degree for adults were ready to abandon some of the past, which often seemed out of date or irrelevant, and replace it with new ways of carrying out the basic procedures of higher education. But those who now take seriously the potential of the assessment degree are willing to be highly inventive in separating these procedures from one another, in trying major new forms of learning, and in emphasizing the accomplishments of the learner, however they may have been gained.

Models

As interest in the external degree developed during the 1960s and particularly as CPEP, CLEP, and other facilitative programs were adopted, it seemed important to bring this potential movement into more coherent focus. A major step in this direction occurred when Jack N. Arbolino of the College Entrance Examination Board and John R. Valley of the Educational Testing Service produced a full-scale model of a third-generation, completely nontraditional assessment degree program to be offered by a "National Commission for the Certification of Accomplishment in Higher Education."[5] The authors held no brief for the title of this organi-

[4] P. L. Dressel (Ed.), *The New Colleges: Toward an Appraisal* (Iowa City: American College Testing Program, 1971), p. 1.

[5] *A Plan for the Study of the Promise and the Problems of an External Degree* and *The Need, the Issues, and the Strategy: A Companion Paper to a Plan for the Study of the Promise and the Problems of an External Degree* (Princeton, N.J.: Educational Testing Service, 1970).

zation and suggested a number of alternatives, their favorite being
"The National University." The two staff documents in which this
model was suggested were not intended for wide distribution, but
their creativeness and concreteness made a strong appeal to influential national leaders who read them. Valley also began the publication of periodic lists of external degree programs and proposals, and
the "Valley Inventory," as it is called, proved to be an important
reference for institutions which wished to consider external degree
programs. (The most recent edition is particularly comprehensive
and rich in detail.[6])

By July 1971, so many institutions were seeking advice on
their proposed programs that the CEEB and ETS established an
Office of External Degree Plans. In the first eleven months of its
operation, it received more than 775 letters of inquiry from all parts
of the country and a broad spectrum of institutions and individuals,
including 167 state systems or individual universities, 129 colleges,
and 48 community colleges. In the summer of 1972 the name of the
Office was changed to Office of New Degree Programs, in part to
indicate that developments in the field had moved from planning
to implementation; by January 1973 the mailing list of the Office
had grown to approximately 1,400 names.

Another significant event in 1971 was the creation by CEEB
and ETS of the Commission on Non-Traditional Study, financed
by a grant from the Carnegie Corporation of New York. The Commission has reported its findings separately and, as noted in the ac-
knowledgements, supported the preparation of this present volume
as an independent enterprise of the author. One of the subcom-
mittees of the Commission gave particular attention to the external
degree and defined six general models which were subsequently refined and described by Valley.[7] His is the best-known effort to tax-
onomize external degrees of the three kinds described here and
therefore is summarized as an introduction to the descriptions of
actual programs which follows. (This summary does not do justice
to the richness of illustration which the original account provides.)

        [6] J. R. Valley, *Increasing the Options* (Princeton, N.J.: Educational
Testing Service, 1972).
        [7] Valley, in Gould and Cross. The quoted material on these models
is all taken from Valley's paper on pp. 97–124.

Valley's *administrative-facilitation* model is generally comparable to the extension degree described here. It is one in which a degree-granting and instructional institution undertakes "to serve the needs of a different clientele yet . . . holds to its customary degree pattern."

His *modes-of-learning* model is comparable to the adult degree. Here an institution "establishes a new degree pattern of learning and teaching that seeks to adjust to the capacities, circumstances, and interests of a different clientele" such as adults.

His *examination, validation,* and *credits* models are refinements of the assessment degree. In the *examination* model, an institution or agency "which need not itself offer instruction" awards credits and degrees based upon student performance on examinations. In the *validation* model, an institution or agency evaluates the student's learning "by a variety of means"—not only by examination. Here the institution essentially restricts its function to that of certification, although it may offer guidance to individual applicants about ways to meet its requirements. In the *credits* model, an institution or agency "vouches for the quality of student programming" in awarding credits and degrees for work completed elsewhere. Perhaps the best example of this model is the Council for National Academic Awards of England, described in Chapter Two; the sole formal function of the CNAA is certification through scrutiny of how well other institutions are performing the processes of admission, instruction, and evaluation.

Valley's sixth or *complex-systems* model is a combination of the other types in which a degree-granting institution or agency "reshapes its pattern of services in various ways, sometimes by combining various simpler models. . . ."

The purpose of the description of programs in the remainder of this chapter is neither to fit them into Valley's six models nor to use them as examples of the three major categories presented here: extension, adult, and assessment degrees. The intent is to be straightforwardly reportorial, indicating the diversity of approaches evident even in a relatively small number of current programs, showing how the need for the external degree spelled out in Chapter Three is being met and laying a basis for the discussion of issues in Chapters Five and Six. In particular, these new programs are not all third-generation programs leading to assessment degrees. Some are primarily extension-degree in nature; others are largely adult-degree programs.

Regents External Degree

In Chapter One it is noted that Ewald Nyquist was one of the pioneers at Columbia University in making its extension degree more adequately measure the actual accomplishments of the adults served. When he went on to the New York State Education Department and became assistant commissioner for higher education, he did not forget the need to revise the framework of the external degree program to aid those people who could not fit into traditional patterns. For example, in evaluating a proposal from a university in the state for a new external degree, he expressed both "fascination" and "disappointment." He observed, "You start out with a perfectly good purpose; and then, at a particular point, you find that you are going to have to make this program conform, in many respects, to your regular program."[8]

The State Education Department itself made a first contribution to the enlargement of opportunities to secure credit when, with aid from the Ford Foundation, it established a College Proficiency Examination Program (CPEP) in 1963. Each of the tests produced in this program covers the work of one or more semesters of college and is written by faculty members of New York State institutions of higher learning under the guidance of the State Education Department staff and with the help of specialists in evaluation. About thirty such tests exist; and, by the end of 1971, 22,500 persons, 7200 in 1971 alone, had taken them. It was expected that about twelve thousand more would be tested in 1972. The passing of these examinations does not automatically award credit, which must be granted by a degree-awarding institution, but a large number of colleges and universities have shown themselves willing to do so.[9]

[8] Jacobson, p. 107.
[9] All data in the ensuing descriptions of programs, unless otherwise attributed, have been secured from brochures, catalogs, releases and other similar publications as well as from correspondence or conversation with administrators or other staff workers.

Part of the success of the program arises from the great historical and constitutional power of the New York State Education Department. It was founded in 1784 according to the theory that all education, formal and informal, public and private, and at every level of instruction, should be centralized in an all-powerful state body. The institution developed for this purpose is called the University of the State of New York, and the members of its Board of Regents are given a sufficiently lengthy tenure (sixteen years) to free them from immediate external influence. In theory, this University controls everything which has to do with teaching and learning in the state; in practice, it delegates much of its power to other bodies, particularly those which offer higher education. It has the right to confer degrees but prior to 1972 gave only honorary ones. But it has had a long-standing system of examinations for high school subjects and possessed both authority and precedent to extend this system at the collegiate level.

Once the CPEP had proved itself, the next step was to award degrees based on the passing of these examinations. In his inaugural address in 1970 as president and commissioner, Nyquist announced that the time had arrived to do so. He was, he said, "proposing to the Board of Regents that The University of the State of New York award undergraduate degrees to those who are able to demonstrate that they possess knowledge and abilities equivalent to those of a degree recipient from a New York State college or university, regardless of how the candidates had prepared themselves." The new degrees, he said, would not compete with those awarded by colleges and universities in the customary fashion but would "serve those citizens who are, for whatever reason, unable to attend institutions of higher learning as resident students." Moreover, he hoped that "success in this venture will stimulate New York's colleges and universities to use their great resources in expanding their own programs for the extension of educational opportunity."[10]

In the program (funded by the Carnegie Corporation and the Ford Foundation) which evolved in early 1971 from this recom-

[10] E. Nyquist, *The Idea of the University of the State of New York* 'Albany, N.Y.: State Education Department, 1970), pp. 7–8.

mendation, three degrees were initially planned: the Associate in
Arts to be conferred beginning in 1972; the Bachelor of Science in
Business Administration to be conferred beginning in 1973; and the
Associate in Applied Science in Nursing in 1973–1974. (The first
77 A.A. degrees were duly awarded in 1972.) Plans for an A.B.
program were announced early in 1973 and presumably other degrees will be developed subsequently. The program is administered
within the department by the Division of Independent Study, of
which Donald J. Nolan is director.

     According to announced plans, the Regents External Degree
is highly flexible. There are no entrance requirements based on previous educational attainment, age, or place of residence. No formal
instruction is offered, but a carefully developed curriculum (based
on fairly conventional patterns of concentration and distribution of
subject matter with some electives) is outlined for each degree.
Guides, bibliographies, and examination descriptions are available
to present or potential enrollees. Students may study in any way
they choose, and their accomplishment is assessed by: course grades;
CPEP, CLEP, and other college-level examinations; United States
Armed Forces Institute transcripts; military courses as evaluated by
CASE; and (as soon as suitable systems are perfected) assessment
of the college-level knowledge acquired through life experience.
Students whose existing credentials do not fit the established degree
requirements are guided in ways to remedy their deficiencies, including attendance at colleges available to them. When a student
is enrolled and his work evaluated, a continuing record of his accomplishments is kept; and, if he requests, transcripts will be fur-
nished to other institutions.

     The Department of Higher Education of the state of New
Jersey is working closely with the New York State authorities and
has established Thomas A. Edison College, which will operate in
much the same way as the New York Regents External Degree Program, thus extending the scope of available opportunities for learning and providing a regional basis for the external degree program.

     Because of the prior existence of CPEP, many people have
assumed that the Regents External Degree is awarded solely on the
passage of examinations and is therefore an adaptation of the London program and an example of Valley's examination model. While

it is only natural that examinations are stressed in the early days of the program, the basic plan seems to fit Valley's validation model in that it uses a broad range of methods of evaluation. Also, unlike the London program, no matriculation standards are set.

The Regents External Degree drastically changes four of the procedures traditionally associated with American higher education and may well change the fifth. Formal admission requirements are abandoned, all effective methods of learning are accepted as valid, varied methods (both old and new) of measuring accomplishment are used, and the degree is awarded by what is as much a department of government as was the University of London until 1900. As plans mature for a degree in nursing, the question of state licensure will inevitably become significant, particularly when graduates wish to practice in states other than New York which do not have non-traditional external degrees. Thus this program breaks profoundly with the past so far as every major procedural point is concerned.

SUNY–Empire State

The publicly supported colleges and universities of New York State (excluding those in New York City) were federated in 1948 into a new entity called the State University of New York, a body which now has seventy-two campuses varying in size and function. Some of these institutions had for many years sponsored pioneering and imaginative programs, including the extension degree. Perhaps the best known of these were the degrees offered by Millard Fillmore College of SUNY-Buffalo. During the chancellorship of Samuel B. Gould, from 1964 to 1970, a striking growth occurred both in the number of institutions and in the non-traditional educational activities which they sponsored.

But while the innovativeness of many other ventures at SUNY is well worth studying, attention is focussed here on Empire State College, created specifically to provide an external degree program. The College was founded by the Board of Trustees of SUNY and by its chancellor, Ernest L. Boyer; the initial funds were provided by the Carnegie Corporation and the Ford Foundation early in 1971. While the resources of the whole educational system of

SUNY are available to Empire State, it has its own small corps of administrators and faculty members, headed by the president, James W. Hall. Its coordinating headquarters are located in Saratoga Springs, but the college also maintains area learning centers throughout the state to which students have access and where most of their direct contact with the institution occurs. The eventual number of these learning centers is not yet set, and their purposes will vary in terms of their clienteles. For example, one of them in the center of Manhattan, offers special services for labor union members who desire to broaden their education. Other centers—such as those in existence or planned for at Albany, Rochester, and Binghamton—will reflect the pattern of needs and desires in their communities.

The college awards the A.A., A.S., B.A., and B.S. degrees. The prospective student must be a high school graduate (of any age), hold an equivalency certificate, or be able to demonstrate the capacity to do advanced work. Previous credit or credit equivalents (such as CPEP or CLEP scores) are taken into account in granting advanced standing. The most important elements in admission, however, are that the student understand thoroughly the nature of the College, be aware of how its program operates, and demonstrate a willingness to undertake independent and usually self-directed study. This understanding is fostered by consultation with a learning-center staff member and by attendance at an orientation workshop. After admission, the student plans his first unit of work; and, when it starts, he is regarded as having been formally matriculated.

Learning can occur in any or all of six modes. (1) *Formal courses* offered by any kind of institution, not merely by colleges or universities. Empire State itself does not offer courses. (2) *Cooperative studies,* in which several students with similar interests work together collaboratively. (3) *Tutorials,* in which a teacher guides an individual student studying a particular area of knowledge or competence. (4) *Organized self-instructional programs,* such as correspondence courses, programmed learning, or televised instruction. (5) *Direct experience,* which may be supervised or unsupervised, but permits self-examination and reflection by the student. (6) *Independent study* by reading, writing, travel, or other means.

The student begins a program at any time during the year by developing, in consultation with a mentor at the center, a contract which describes what he proposes to do during a specific period of time to achieve a learning goal or goals. The activities proposed may be selected from one or all of the modes and are tailored to the resources available to the student. A number of illustrations of contracts have been published by the College in its catalog so the student can have models for evolving his own plan. A part of each contract specifies how the student will be evaluated, both while he is carrying out his plan and at its conclusion. Generally speaking, each contract is part of a larger program of study upon which the student and mentor have agreed but which can change with the passage of time. If a student is preparing for entry into a graduate or professional school, it is expected that the program of study will be constructed with that fact in mind.

The mentor who guides this process is an academically trained person who has had experience as a faculty member. He may work full-time for Empire State (on either a permanent or term basis) or be a faculty member at another college or university. The role of the mentor is "to help students clarify their purposes, develop a general conceptual framework for program planning, make specific plans for study, and evaluate their progress. A student usually works with mentors whose areas of competence and interest fit the student's purposes." During the course of the individual contract and as the program of study takes firmer shape, "the mentor helps the student evaluate its effectiveness and renders his own judgements concerning the student's performance in the various learning activities undertaken. For a portion of some contracts the mentor also will be a tutor for those areas of knowledge and competence which he can meet."[11]

The organizing framework for the degree may be vocational/professional, disciplinary/interdisciplinary, problem oriented, or holistic/thematic. The first category has to do with recognized occupations. The disciplines are those customary to a college, such as economics, fine arts, history, or mathematics. The problem orientations have to do with such topics as population, environment, race, civil liberties, transportation, or world peace. The holistic/thematic programs deal with such topics as the culture of cities, the culture of work, or the fine arts and society.

[11] *Interim Report 1971–1972* (n.p.: Empire State College, n.d.).

The general policy of the College is that a "degree is awarded when the student completes a program of study which the faculty supports, at a level of competence which meets College standards. In general, formal credit study undertaken at accredited colleges will be completely transferable. Expectations for a typical high school graduate normally call for eighteen months of full-time study or its equivalent for the [associate] degree, and thirty-six months of full-time study for the [baccalaureate] degree. Every student will complete a minimum program of study with Empire State of not less than three months duration for the [associate degree] and six months for the [baccalaureate degree]."[12]

As the student nears the end of his program and usually just before the start of what he and his mentor believe will be the final contract, a review committee of the administration and faculty of the College goes over his total record in order to approve the contract, to suggest changes in it, or to require further work. When these requirements have been met, the total record is reviewed at the Coordinating Center; if it is approved, the student is recommended for a degree.

In the Empire State program, virtually everything differs from normal college practice at each stage—from admission to certification. Some customary terms, such as mentor, contract, and mode of study, have been given new meanings which have already achieved widespread currency. It is interesting to observe, however, that while the traditional concept of residence is abandoned, the requirement concerning length of full-time study or its equivalent still remains an overall determinant of the scope of the degree; as with virtually all other colleges, the student must spend a prescribed amount of time in contact with Empire State College in order to receive its degree.

Minnesota Metropolitan State College

While the Minnesota Metropolitan State College (MMSC) has many noteworthy features, the one which catches the attention of most observers is its total reliance on the metropolitan area it serves

[12] *Interim Report.*

for physical facilities, for the cultural enrichment of its students, and for many of its faculty who, while fully qualified academically, have their chief employment elsewhere than at the institution.[13] The College comes to terms with a pro-city bias by insisting that instruction be undertaken in the underutilized facilities of schools, libraries, museums, churches, parks, and commercial institutions. Also, while the institution has a necessary core of full-time faculty members and administrators, there are about ten times as many "community faculty members."

MMSC was designed to collaborate with existing institutions to serve the clientele they were not reaching. The outside observer might be excused for thinking that Minnesota—and particularly the Twin Cities area—was already adequately served by institutions of higher education. In addition to twenty-four private colleges and universities, the state had in 1970 four systems of postsecondary education: the University of Minnesota, centered in the Twin Cities; six well-established state colleges under the control of the State College Board; eighteen junior colleges, six of them in the seven-county metropolitan area; and thirty-one area vocational-technical schools, including six in the metropolitan area.

It seemed clear, however, to the State College Board and its chancellor, G. Theodore Mitau, that an upperdivisional college was needed in the Twin Cities area. A proposal to create such a college was first made in 1968 but was not accepted by the legislature. During the next two years, the proposal was studied and approved by the Citizens' League, an influential group in the metropolitan area; and, in 1971, authorization to create the College and an appropriation for its planning was passed by the legislature and approved by the governor. Subsequently, additional funds have been granted by the Carnegie Corporation and other foundations. Thus a seventh state college was added to the responsibilities of the State College Board.

MMSC came into existence on a wave of public approval. In August 1971, the Minneapolis Star conducted a poll of its readers on the novel arrangements proposed. It found that "nine out

[13] An excellent summary account of this program is given by D. Sweet, "A Model for an Upper-division Urban College," in Vermilye, pp. 211–224.

of ten interviewed by Metro-Poll think the new school's plan to operate year-round and on weekends sounds like a solid idea. Eight of ten think it will be beneficial to have professionals not trained as teachers giving instruction in their specialties. Two of three approve of using other facilities than traditional classrooms for instruction. In sum, 72 percent think the new college will 'fill a need that other state colleges have not filled.' "[14]

MMSC has defined its audience in very clear terms. Its founding president, David Sweet, has pointed out that it

> serves a student body that is beyond the traditional age group of seventeen to twenty-one or eighteen to twenty-two —the immediate post–high school graduate. Seventy-five percent of MMSC's students are over twenty-five. In addition, the college is committed to provide educational opportunities for the poor, minority groups, and women. Specifically, the students whom MMSC serves are adults who have dropped out of college but who have the potential and desire to complete college degrees; adults who have acquired the equivalent of the first two years of college through work or other experiences including military service; adults who require collegiate-level retraining to meet their personal or professional goals and to cope with the technological demands of the changing economy; adults who transfer from one of the six metropolitan area junior colleges; adults who have completed post–secondary courses in area vocational-technical schools; and adults whose unique higher education needs have not been met by other institutions.[15]

The student who wishes to enroll must have completed two or more years of satisfactory work (with at least a C-average) at another college or university or be able to demonstrate an equivalent amount of education by other means. Students may apply at any time of the year. They receive extensive counseling and guidance as well as pamphlets which explain the program in clear terms. They then join an orientation group which probes deeply into its

[14] *Minneapolis Star,* October 20, 1971.
[15] Sweet, p. 212.

members' understanding of the program and the readiness of each one to undertake it. Anyone whose interest continues is assigned to a permanent faculty advisor with whom he has primary contact throughout the program. A special Assessment, Advising, and Contracting Committee is appointed (made up of both faculty and students); under its guidance, the student develops a degree contract (sometimes called a pact) which includes a full plan for the total educational program to be undertaken. This contract is examined by a Contract Review Committee, also made up of faculty and students, which may require revisions before acceptance.

The degree contract, which the student is fully responsible for initiating and carrying out, should show how an appropriate level of competency is to be achieved and demonstrated in each of five areas which the College has defined as essential. Each has been fully defined in the College's literature and the level required depends upon the student concerned. Stated very briefly, the competency areas are: (1) *Basic learning skills* (includes the ability to find and use information and resources, to identify one's learning needs and plan a strategy to meet them, to write coherently, to communicate effectively orally, to comprehend written information, to listen with discrimination, and to handle general computational tasks); (2) *Civic skills* (includes an understanding of the urban community, the student's interrelationship with it, and the skill to work with other people toward social goals); (3) *Cultural-recreational competencies* (includes an awareness of the many products and activities of civilization—literature, the fine arts, the humanities—and the ability to share in them creatively); (4) *Vocational competencies* (includes the possession of one or more marketable skills, not merely an awareness of the world of work); (5) *Personal and social awareness* (includes an assessment of the individual as he sees himself and as he thinks others see him and a realization and tolerance of individual differences).

In designing the degree contract, the student is helped by the advisor and the committees which review the plan of study to identify the best learning resources available. As new community resources are found, the range will constantly broaden. The courses taught by the College itself are so scheduled and located as to be available to a maximum number of students who might profit from them. Any student proposing an unusual way of meeting a requirement may draw up a project contract to be approved by the advisor.

The completion of the program comes as soon as the student feels ready for it. When he believes he has completed his degree contract, he requests the appointment of a Final Assessment Committee and prepares for it evidence of achievement at the level set. Usually this statement is set forth in the form of a narrative account incorporating all available evidence of the work done. The Committee takes this final task of assessment very seriously; and may work with the student in a number of ways to test the actual accomplishment of goals. For, as the president of the College says, "The key to our educational program is assessment. We believe that the competence-assessment process—both initially and throughout the student's affiliation with the college, including the assessment which will culminate in his receiving a degree—should be individually structured to give the student a complete opportunity to demonstrate his real abilities. The function of assessment is not to fail students but to make sure they have the skills and knowledge, the values and attitudes, and the understanding—in short, the competencies—which are appropriate to their educational, career, and life goals."[16] Any student who cannot satisfy the Final Assessment Committee of a satisfactory level of competence is permitted to continue until he reaches the point when he can do so.

The MMSC degree plan is an experimental one, and, if it succeeds, other programs (already being considered by the leaders of the institution) may be developed. Among them might be certificate programs, specialized baccalaureates, and graduate study at the master's level.

Florida International University

Within the Florida State University system, nine universities controlled by a single board and chancellor, a special degree for adults is already offered at the University of South Florida at Tampa. However, the responsibility for providing an assessment degree has been allocated by the board and Chancellor Robert B. Mauz to Florida International University, a new comprehensive

[16] Sweet, p. 222.

university (beginning with the junior undergraduate year) in the heavily populated Miami area. This new degree will be offered by a School of Independent Studies of which Jules O. Pagano is Dean of Special Programs.

An upperdivisional external degree program for the baccalaureate is offered to all Florida residents. Presently a degree may be secured in the humanities, labor and manpower studies, urban and environmental economics, urban sociology, urban politics, the social and behavioral sciences of nursing and other health-care fields, welfare, urban justice, or general business. For each degree program, there are areas of concentration and electives adding up to ninety credit hours of work. Applicants are interviewed in depth on the Miami campus or by members of teams which travel throughout the state. The student and his program advisor then devise an "education contract plan" for fulfilling the requirements for a degree, either by courses at available institutions or by other acceptable means, and for evaluating the student's accomplishment.

Strong administrative backing is provided for this program by President Charles E. Perry, who refers to Florida International as "The Continuing Education University" and believes it to be a "rebirth of the land-grant tradition which provided competent service to our citizens in order to meet their educational needs, whenever and wherever they arose."[17] Since the new University is in an urban area and the whole state is rapidly becoming urbanized, both the external-degree program and other educational services must be shaped to the needs and desires of city-dwellers. The non-tradiional external degree will be surrounded and reinforced by a cluster of other services which will not merely inform potential students about the values of the degree but will also provide many other educative experiences.

Community College of Vermont

It is often difficult to determine precisely what an external degree means so far as a community college is concerned; its range

[17] C. E. Perry, *The Continuing Education University.* An address presented at Michigan State University, November 1, 1971. Publisher and date unstated, pages unnumbered.

of services may be so broad that distinctions between "resident" or "full-time" students and those who study in specially designed sequences or in patterns created to their own wishes and necessities are hard to make. More than that, a community college often begins by being wholly "external." A lag, sometimes of several years, occurs from the time a faculty is assembled and is finally moved into the physical facilities built for it. During that interval, the instructional and administrative staff may keep themselves occupied, at least in part, by teaching courses for adults, often in borrowed quarters. When the new physical plant is occupied, however, the program tends toward regularization and toward the establishment of some distinctions between the internal and the external students, though the differences are seldom as great as in other institutions of higher education.

At the Community College of Vermont (CCV), however, the total pattern of instruction is external. The institution, which did not enter the planning stage until 1970, is designed as a single administrative structure, administered from Montpelier by the Vermont Regional Community College System and directed by Peter P. Smith. However, CCV has regional site offices (using high schools, state colleges, or other similar facilities) in various sections of the state. Each site has an administrative and counseling staff, whose members are trained for and supervised in their duties and who develop programs which, in their judgment, best suit the needs of their constituencies. The College—which is designed primarily for a rural population which could not otherwise achieve a college education—is funded primarily from Office of Economic Opportunity and other federal grants, though it also receives funds from the Carnegie Corporation.

CCV offers certificates of various sorts for those not wishing to secure degrees, but its primary emphasis is upon the Associate degree. No level of educational achievement is required for entry, and great attention is paid to the creation of an individualized pattern of courses. All students who apply are admitted, but they are expected to undergo a substantial amount of orientation and counseling (either individual or group) both before they begin study and subsequently. Each student is encouraged to take any available courses which seem interesting and relevant; sometimes this period of exploration is lengthy, sometimes it is short. Great attention is paid to ongoing as well as end-of-course evaluation, and teachers are urged to seek feedback from their students. At the end of the period, the teacher prepares a certificate of achievement for each student reflecting the extent to which the objectives of the course have been met and the nature of the in-process evaluation. This certificate becomes part of the student's records; only successfully completed courses are entered.

When the student feels that the process of exploration is over, he works out with a counselor a contract to complete the program. This contract includes learning experiences prior to enrollment and courses taken at CCV. It reflects a personal-need assessment as well as the achievement of fifteen competencies within three major areas defined by the college: intellectual, social, and physical/manual. This contract must be approved by the Regional Site Review Committee. Upon completion of the contract to the satisfaction of the counselor and the Committee, as well as of a CCV Review Board, the degree is awarded.

In designing the structure and program of CCV, a broad base of involvement has been worked out with the people of the state; it includes a statewide Commission of eighteen members, a number of State Advisory Councils in various content areas, and part-time staff and faculty members who (while academically qualified for their teaching or other roles in the College) are drawn from a wide range of occupations and backgrounds.

Extended University of the University of California

The University of California is well known for the complexity of the interlocking systems of authority on its nine campuses. Consequently its movement toward an external degree has been a slow and cautious one; in the long run, however, the great strength of the institution may generate a powerful and varied cluster of programs. The idea of an external degree was first set before an All-University Faculty Conference in March 1970, by President Charles A. Hitch; finding that his proposal was generally approved, he appointed an all-University Task Force of fifteen broadly representative faculty members and administrators to consider the matter, with Leonard Freedman of UCLA as chairman. A preliminary report of this task force to the key groups in the University indicated their general approval of the idea, but reactions from the chancellors and the Academic Senate committees clarified and altered several points. In September 1971, the regents approved $250,-000 for planning and early development of what had come to be called the "Extended University." The final report of the task force was issued in November 1971, with fifty-four recommendations calling for sweeping changes in the degree-awarding systems of the University.[18]

It became clear, however, that no bold steps were to be taken immediately. In 1970 and 1971, some people had talked about the Extended University as a "tenth campus," but the nine existing campuses naturally were not favorable to this idea, particularly since any all-state program would cut across their geographic areas of service and might also cause some restriction of their budgets. The Freedman Committee, as one of its major recommendations, called for the creation of a University-wide "consortium of the campuses" to be called "New College," having not only stimulative and coordinative powers but also the right to confer degrees, either separately or in conjunction with one of the existing campuses. This consortium was duly established on July 1, 1972, but its central function is that of working with and through the existing campus authorities, a policy initiated by David P. Gardner, vice-president, Extended Academic and Public Service Programs, who is the executive officer for the Consortium.

As yet, the University has followed the concept of the pilot program with each of the nine campuses evolving a pattern of work which its authorities feel best suited to the time and place. In the academic year 1972–1973, eleven programs were at the stage of initiation or planning: seven involving either the bachelor's or the master's degree, three providing services for experimental groups, and one the planning stage of an as-yet-undefined program.

The new degrees are almost entirely extension degrees following Valley's administrative-facilitation model. (Here the term *extension degree* is used as defined in this book and not in terms of

[18] *Degree Programs for the Part-Time Student* (Berkeley: University of California Press, 1971).

certain administrative distinctions made at the University.) Berkeley, for example, is offering the Master of Business Administration degree in the financial district of San Francisco. For the most part, the admission standards, the program of courses, and the faculty will be the same as on campus. Essentially the same policies are followed in the M.B.A. program at UCLA, the Master of Administration program at Riverside, the Master of Science in Electrical Engineering at Santa Barbara, and in other degree programs. On several campuses, such as at Davis, Riverside, and San Diego, the plan is to admit a limited number of part-time students, in some cases rescheduling campus courses to the evening hours so that they can be taken by both full-time and part-time students.

The program seen as a whole appears rather conventional, and one cynical faculty member at Berkeley observed that the University "is marching forward boldly into the 1920s." Closer study reveals, however, that efforts are being made to adapt features of several programs to incorporate non-traditional elements. Thus it is said, both at Berkeley and at UCLA, that, in the admission of students, attention will be paid to the amount and nature of each applicant's work experience. An unpublished statement concerning the Berkeley M.B.A. notes that "to be admitted to the downtown program, a student must have completed undergraduate courses in microeconomics, macroeconomics, elementary accounting, elementary statistics, and mathematics through calculus. This background will permit some condensation of work which on-campus students take in their first year." Other novelties are: new curricula (as at Irvine and Santa Barbara); and the use in some programs of audiotapes, videotapes, programmed instruction, intercampus telecommunications, and closed-circuit television. The directors of some programs plan to experiment with short residential courses and seminars and also to identify off-campus places where learning centers might be located.

Plans exist to evaluate existing and future proposals and programs carefully, to make studies of potential clienteles, and, through the Consortium, to build a sense of collaborative effort which will strengthen the Extended University and make it at once more responsive to the needs of the state and more dynamically a center of experimentation for the system as a whole. The Freedman Report has not been fully implemented, but it serves as a guide which some administrative and academic leaders are taking seriously. If substantial new funds are provided for the Extended University—which appears likely as this book goes to press—innovative programming can be more rapidly undertaken.

California State University and Colleges

The history of the external degree at The California State University and Colleges (CSUC) parallels in many of its essentials the aims and efforts of the University of California degree. In January 1971, Chancellor Glenn S. Dumke of CSUC put forward a systemwide plan for non-traditional degree programs to supplement the extension and part-time offerings then in existence. Receiving an enthusiastic response, he appointed a Commission on External Degree Programs, chaired by President Thomas H. McGrath of California State College, Sonoma, and made up of nine administrators from various campuses, to study the idea and put forward plans. Late in 1971, this Committee sponsored a statewide conference with speakers from both California and other parts of the country. This conference and the resulting report were entitled *The 1,000-Mile Campus*,[19] and this term has become something of a slogan for the CSUC external-degree effort.

Plans were developed by the Commission and approved by the various CSUC authorities. The Commission remains in existence to effectuate its plans and hopes that by about 1975, its guiding and controlling function will be over and its work integrated into established patterns of academic administration. It has evolved a special definition of external degrees as "self-support programs of instruction and assessment leading to regularly established degrees of The California State University and Colleges. They will be upper division and graduate programs designed to serve adult Californians for whom degree and certificate programs are not now available because of their inability to spend extensive periods of time in residence on a college campus."

In accordance with this definition, the Commission has established criteria governing the activities it sponsors, the central idea being that they shall be carefully evaluated pilot programs. In

[19] Published by the Office of the Chancellor.

1972–1973, six of the nineteen colleges and universities sponsored
ten programs, six of which award the bachelor's degree and the
rest the master's degree. These programs are, on the whole, highly
conventional in form, using the classroom lecture-discussion approach to instruction and concerning such occupational fields as
business or public administration. Only one of the programs, a master's degree in humanistic psychology offered at Sonoma, makes
extensive use of unconventional methods of learning and evaluation
such as instructional plans developed by the student and his counselor using the resources of the community as well as of the campus
and requiring an ultimate review of accomplishment by an Examination Board.

The Commission has made sampling studies in the north
San Francisco Bay counties and in Los Angeles and Orange counties of the market for the external degree and estimates a potential
and immediate clientele of about seventy-two thousand Californians.
The group is also exploring plans for a credit exchange (in which a
cumulative record might be kept for the student of all his verified
learning accomplishments), a system of "self-reliant" study, special
programs adapted to the needs of minorities and the poor, and a
consortium of the nineteen campuses which would have the right
to award its own degree. The extent to which these plans will be
activated remains to be seen.

The two powerful university systems and the community
college system of California as yet have not come to any accom-
modation on the matter of the external degree, a fact which has not
gone unnoted in the state. (Why, for example, should there be two
separate statewide consortiums for the same purpose?) Meanwhile,
the rhetoric of certain academic figures within all three systems
promises much innovation. Perhaps, in due time, by leadership from
within and pressure from without, external degrees will become far
more common in California than they are now.

University Without Walls

For many people, the term *university without walls* has a
generic meaning, loosely symbolizing all external-degree activities
or even all extramural teaching. Thus the U.S. Department of

Housing and Urban Development often calls its National Urban Studies Program a university without walls.[20] Broad usage of this term blurs a proper understanding of the program which has that specific name and which has a powerful independent vitality.

The University Without Walls (UWW) is sponsored by the Union for Experimenting Colleges and Universities, an association which in February 1972, had twenty-five institutional members. Eighteen were taking part in the UWW, along with two non-Union colleges and universities. The Union, which has its headquarters at Antioch College, Yellow Springs, Ohio, and whose president is Samuel Baskin, came into existence in 1964 as a way of cooperatively conducting innovation and experimentation in college teaching. The Union works in a number of ways; for example, it helped plan the development of *Change* magazine (which describes and interprets the practices and processes of innovation in higher education), it conducts summer workshops for college teachers, and it has conducted studies on the student protest movement and strategies for innovation in higher education.

UWW is unique in that it was originated by and will continue to be refined by faculty members of the collaborating institutions. In summer workshops beginning in 1967 and continuing through 1969, professors from colleges in the Union drew up increasingly precise proposals for freeing their institutions from the traditions of the internal degree and for creating new and more responsive ways to serve their communities. A proposal was written in 1969 by the Union's staff, and substantial funding was secured in 1970, including $400,000 each from the U.S. Office of Education and the Ford Foundation.

An excellent in-depth description of the program is presented in the first major report of its activities;[21] the following is a very brief summary of material chiefly drawn from that report. The institutions concerned represent a broad spectrum of colleges and universities and include: Antioch College; Bard College; Chicago

[20] For a description of this program, see the report by M. W. Wachs in *The 1,000-Mile Campus*, pp. 37–39, 74.

[21] Union for Experimenting Colleges and Universities, *The University Without Walls: A First Report* (Yellow Springs, O.: Antioch College, 1972).

State University; Friends World College; Goddard College; Howard University; Loretto Heights College; Morgan State College; New College (Sarasota, Florida); New York University; Northeastern Illinois University; Roger Williams College; Shaw University; Skidmore College; Staten Island Community College; Stephens College; the University of Massachusetts; the University of Minnesota; the University of South Carolina; and Westminster College.

Although many of these institutions cluster along the eastern seaboard, sufficient diversity exists to make the Union a truly national consortium. Each campus has developed its distinctive program for the baccalaureate using task forces of faculty members, administrators, and students. The policies for selection of students are also left up to each unit, though in general no lower or upper age barriers are imposed, and the First Report notes that admission might be based on "such criteria as student motivation, creativity, independence, job history, and previous life experiences . . . rather than test scores and grades in school."

For the most part, the program is individualized, beginning with a process of orientation followed by the identification by the student and his teacher-adviser of a plan of action using different kinds of experience chosen from an Inventory of Learning Resources built up at each institution. The student proceeds at a pace determined by his abilities and by the availability of the resources to be used, keeping a cumulative record of learning plans and accomplishments. When he feels ready to present himself for a degree, the final evaluation of his work is made by a review committe of faculty members, students, and others with whom the student has been working.

Sharp criticisms have been made of the intellectual integrity of much of the work allowed in this program and in others which follow its general plan. Herbert London has suggested, for example, that students involved in the plan become knowledgeable about which faculty members are likely to give credit without exacting heavy requirements—not, it might be noted, a previously unknown practice in higher education. One young man was given six credits of advanced standing in physical education because he said he had taught swimming in a club; a young woman secured a degree in beekeeping using her father, a beekeeper, as a mentor. (What she

did, she said, was to stay at home and give her dad some help.)
But, as London points out, other institutions and faculty advisers
adhere to rigorous standards,[22] and both the UWW and the Union
are devoting a great deal of attention to more vigorous evaluation,
documentation, and research.

While all of the programs described in this chapter operate
in terms of a governing theory, UWW (perhaps because of a long
period of advance preparation by faculty members) has developed
eight organizing concepts which are described in depth in its First
Report but which are given here only in brief form. In a sense, they
present the propositions underlying many programs which award
non-traditional external degrees, even those whose processes differ
substantially from those of the UWW:

> *Many persons beyond the usual age range for col-*
> *lege would like to have and would profit from a college ed-*
> *ucation. Many of them have acquired much skill and knowl-*
> *edge from their life experiences. A mix of ages, in which*
> *younger and older persons interact, would benefit all.*
>
> *A criticism that figured large in campus protests was*
> *that students have seldom been sufficiently involved in the*
> *design and governance of colleges. It is clear that students*
> *are less resistant to programs they themselves have helped*
> *to devise and to operate. Also students gain important knowl-*
> *edge and experience from understanding the issues that the*
> *faculty and administration must confront. Working together*
> *helps to heal destructive breaches.*
>
> *Most students come to college unprepared for self-*
> *directed study. For the most part the planning and direc-*
> *tion of their educational experiences has been determined*
> *by others. Too often they have been told what to do and*
> *when, where, and how to do it. A major challenge for higher*
> *education is to help students overcome their dependence*
> *and to achieve confidence in setting and pursuing their own*
> *educational goals.*
>
> *No two students are exactly alike in their back-*

[22] Herbert London, "University Without Walls: Reform or Rip-
Off?" *Saturday Review,* September 16, 1972, p. 62–66.

ground, educational aptitudes, interests, and needs. Wasteful "lock-step" methods must be replaced by adaptation to the individual student—taking into account his long-term and short-term goals. Students are likely to be more highly motivated and their education programs are likely to take on more meaning when these programs are designed by and for the student as a unique person.

There are many ways in which students can learn; the traditional college class in which the professor lectures or leads discussion is one way. Students also learn from their own firsthand experiences; from friends; from employers or supervisors; from television, radio, films, newspapers, magazines, books, travel, and interaction in various cultures and subcultures.

Many persons outside the regular educational institution can contribute significantly to students' undergraduate experience. Limiting educational leadership to the faculty of the colleges and universities deprives students of working with those men and women who are outstanding in their own roles and able to give students the most up-to-date viewpoints. Any society should include among its educators its best artists, scientists, writers, musicians, dancers, physicians, lawyers, clergymen, industrialists, financiers, and other specialists.

Not even the largest "multiversity" can offer all the resources needed by students today. One possibility, in our mobile society, is freedom for the student to go wherever he is likely to find what he needs. In addition, the student's education may be greatly enhanced if he can be part of the "mix" of more than one educational institution.

Traditional assessment procedures (time spent in the classroom, course credits, grades, achievement tests on prescribed subject matter) do not reveal enough about the individual's growth and development. This is likely to be especially true in the UWW program, where students are working in many different ways and settings . . . One crucial task of the UWW program will be to find new approaches to evaluation that will periodically appraise the individual's cognitive and affective learning for the student and his adviser.

Many institutions of higher learning have applied to join the UWW and even more have inquired about the feasibility of doing so. Its ultimate constituency may grow very large, particularly since it has a grant of funds from UNESCO to conduct planning sessions in several European countries to explore the feasibility of the UWW concept abroad.

Central New York Regional Learning Service

In 1969, in a series of Founders' Lectures at Colgate University, Samuel B. Gould proposed a radical concept called a *communiversity*. "The university of the future," he said, "will be a loose federation of all the educational and cultural forces of a community—at every age level. It will be a coordinated educational entity serving a single, fairly large community or a single, compact region." Such an institution, as he envisions it, will break away from existing hierarchies and patterns and in time "will integrate all the community's resources to the intellectual and aesthetic needs of its people. It will offer a greater hope to all minority groups than they can look to within present structures. It is bound to cause some sort of teaching or educational and cultural involvement from nearly everyone as both a learner or a preceptor. It will offer presently lacking strength to the community's cultural agencies, because they will be part of the regular pattern of education and will, therefore, be more willingly supported."[23]

Initial testing of this conception was undertaken in 1971 when the Policy Institute of the Syracuse University Research Corporation received two grants from the Ford Foundation to finance an in-depth exploration of the educational facilities in five New York State counties in the Syracuse area. This effort was guided by a consortium made up of the fifteen public and private colleges in the area and of representatives of the Elementary and Secondary

[23] S. B. Gould, *Today's Academic Condition* (New York: McGraw-Hill, 1970), pp. 90–92.

Educational Council of Central New York. Initially Stephen K. Bailey administered the exploration; the present administrator is Francis U. Macy.

The consortium and other institutions (both in the five-county area and elsewhere) made an intensive study of how the unserved student, particularly the adult, could best be helped; and, with the aid of staff-written and commissioned papers, a plan gradually evolved for The Central New York Regional Learning Service (RLS), now established by a grant from the U.S. Office of Education. It is hoped that by 1977 RLS will have a client load of about five thousand persons and will be self-supporting. It is further hoped that RLS can offer the same kind of assistance to the seekers of high school diplomas that it gives to those who wish degrees.

The general plan involves three kinds of services, the first of which is *counseling*, a broad term which includes a strongly supportive relationship between the student and locally based learning consultants trained to provide a wide range of diagnostic and advisory services as well as to help individuals set goals for themselves, design patterns of learning activities, and carry them out.

The second service is *facilitation* of the learning undertaken by the students. Ultimately the choice of activities will be guided by the goals set, but the learner and his consultant will be aided by three computerized services. The first is the Educational Resource Directory which includes all educational resources in the region, no matter who sponsors them nor what their method of instruction may be. The second is a Regional Instructional Reserve which lists all local people qualified (in the judgment of academic panels) to serve as tutors. In this way, the talents of highly trained people throughout the community can serve as instructional resources. If the student needs to learn something, the computer can furnish a list of people who can teach it and who are geographically available. The third computerized facilitating service is a Student Monitoring System which stores data on clients, paying particular attention to their educational accomplishments.

The third broad service is the *validation* of academic quality and of the integrity of the overall educational design. The entire RLS will use either already accredited learning resources (such as college or secondary school courses and sequences or established equivalency tests) or monitor other learning experiences or tutors by the use of panels of academic experts.

RLS will not itself give a diploma or a degree but will guide the student to the institution which most nearly meets his learning needs. A degree may be awarded, for example, by one of the colleges or universities in the region or elsewhere, by SUNY-Empire State College, or by the Board of Regents. Thus the Service stands in an intermediary position. It serves the student, often being his advocate as well as his guide. It meshes the work of individual tutors with that of institutions, some of them traditional and some not. It establishes and maintains standards of quality, serving as a bulwark against the cheapness and duplicity which is an endemic danger in unsupervised and unregulated external-degree study.

Miscellany

The programs described in this chapter are but a few of the best-known and most highly developed examples of the non-traditional external degree. Countless others exist. Many of them are noted in Valley's *Increasing the Options;* others are being announced constantly, and administrators and faculty members are at work shaping plans which are not yet ready to be announced.

The example of the Open University has so captured the imaginations of many that several efforts have been made to transplant it, wholly or in part, to the United States. Two partial ventures are now receiving special attention. One is the trial use of some of the OU teaching materials on an optional basis at three American institutions of higher learning: Rutgers University, the University of Houston, and the University of Maryland. This project got under way in 1972–1973, administered by the CEEB and evaluated by ETS with funds granted by the Carnegie Corporation.

The other American parallel, completely indigenous to the United States but resembling the educational design of OU, is the State University of Nebraska (SUN), a cooperative venture of the educational institutions of that state supported by grants from the U.S. Office of Education. SUN is still in a developmental stage but early designs call for the offering of courses by television, radio, correspondence instruction, laboratory kits, videotape, and other materials. Study centers will be set up throughout the state. Initially only courses in the first two years of collegiate instruction will be offered, and a plan for awarding a degree had not been announced at the time this account was written.

Most new American programs take as their point of origin some component of content or service, such as a new curriculum, a concern about students, a new locus of learning, or a new teaching device or strategy. The variety and ingenuity of the ideas for nontraditional degrees have been amazing. Since John Summerskill treats this diversity in some detail in the Epilogue, it will not be dealt with here.

Concluding Note

One feature of the assessment external degree—noted in the concluding section of Chapter Two—is its constitution as a systemwide or consortium degree. While examples exist of unconventional programs of service at individual institutions, the preponderant pattern is otherwise.

Assessment external degrees are created, in fact, in one of two general ways. In the first, a governor, state commissioner, or systemwide chancellor concludes that the geographic area for which he is educationally responsible has needs which must be met by new means. In the second, a consortium of colleges and universities, either formally linked as members in a statewide system or as freestanding institutions, join together to engage in experimentation, pilot programming, and interchange of ideas and staffs. Collective effort of this sort has not been characteristic of either the extension or the adult degree, and perhaps this feature of comprehensive planning and service is a major distinguishing characteristic of the assessment external degree. But while this is undeniably true of the present situation, the condition may be only temporary. More individual colleges and universities may move with boldness into new kinds of degree offerings. And at least some of the new practices in admission, instruction, evaluation, certification, and perhaps licensing are applicable to many forms of higher education and may eventually have a lasting effect on all of it.

5

Institutional

Issues

Where men build on false grounds, the more they build, the greater is the ruine.

THOMAS HOBBES

*P*erhaps the best omen for the success of the assessment external degree is that, in two years of wide discussion, few have regarded it as a panacea. American education at all levels has a certain flighty quality which leads to the consideration by those seeking either novelty or certainty of each new, powerfully backed idea as Heaven's ultimate law. At the first signs of adversity, disillusionment, quickly followed by derision and oblivion, appears.

In the case of the assessment degree, however, even the proposers of the idea suggest it as a new option for unserved degree-seekers rather than as a substitute for present systems, as a way of testing innovation before adoption rather than as a demand for immediate effectuation of new processes, and as an opportunity for creativity in colleges and universities rather than as a prepackaged

120

plan to be uncritically accepted. Even those who cast their lot with the assessment degree warn of its possible excesses. Stephen K. Bailey, after quoting Pifer's comment that the assessment degree is "an idea whose time has come," observes that "if we are not careful, it may be an idea whose time will soon have passed" and notes that "at the bottom of this basket of shiny apples lurk some serpents."[1] (These serpents appear in due course later in this and the following chapter.) This cautious view of possibilities, followed (it is hoped) by careful planning, augurs a more enduring program than does the assumption, so often made in the past, that quick salvation is to be found in a catchily phrased but cloudy concept.

This cautious and concerned approach brings to the fore a number of issues concerning the assessment degree, each of which is identified and explored briefly here. A discussion of these issues necessarily must have a tentative and speculative air. The studies, data, and lore relating to the extension degree are voluminous and have already provided the basis for conclusions not reviewed here except as they are relevant to current issues. But little hard data has yet been produced concerning either the adult degree or the assessment degree. Neither a "right answer" nor a consensus concerning these issues has emerged; and on many it may never appear, since what is right for one institution may be wrong for another.

A rough division can be made between those issues which confront designers of specific programs and those which confront leaders in the field of higher education as a whole—legislators and other policy-makers, administrators, and faculty members. The two groups of issues overlap; the second flows naturally from the first, but each can be seen more clearly if brought into focus separately. Chapter Five considers the institutional issues; the broader issues will be dealt with in Chapter Six.

New Frameworks

The idea for a specific external-degree program may spring from almost any quarter: a politician, a university board member, an administrator, an instructor, an entrepreneur, a member of a

[1] Bailey, pp. 172–173.

pressure group, or a potential student. If the idea is to be taken seriously, either its originator or somebody else must design a program which fully considers policies of admission, teaching, evaluation, and certification. Often this process is repeated several times as other individuals and groups review the proposed program.

If this planning process is thorough, it requires the establishment of new frameworks of thought and practice. The difficulty of solving many problems simultaneously is suggested by one such planner:

> *Within the traditional system you have certain parameters, certain guidelines which are then accepted by everyone. In a new operation none of this exists. What is a full-time equivalent student? How do you decide that? We've had to lay out new guidelines for that essentially, and then build it into our whole contractual format. How do you do such a simple thing as have admissions, or charge tuition, particularly if you're operating without a fixed calendar? Suppose the student just doesn't work out well with a particular tutor, how do you shift, how do you provide for that student to move forward without being penalized for that? What does a faculty member's year look like? We have them on twelve-month contract; how much of that is spent monitoring, how much doing other kinds of preparation? Is it an appointmentlike basis, client-related, or is there a collegial group that has to discuss all these problems? These are absolutely the most stunning academic questions you'd want to deal with. They're very much to the point and represent the real challenge of what we're trying to do.*[2]

The lack of fixed reference-points can lead to the frustration expressed by the director of one program who, when asked "what are your major problems?" answered:

---

[2] This quotation, like all the others in this chapter and Chapter Six, unless otherwise noted, comes from the leadership study described in the Preface.

*The first ones are finance and student recruitment. Another
is the internal agony between the forces of change and the
forces that hold the line, and the ability of people to tolerate
the ambiguity of a new program. Frequently, they want answers even before you're able to ask the question. There's a
tremendous amount of anxiety and unrest and suspicion.
You've got to operate in a political atmosphere which requires a balance between students who want changes to
have happened yesterday and the realities that only the staff
is aware of—for example, the professor over there in psychology or geology or art who's going to blow at the next
faculty assembly. I think the anxiety here over where the
college is going, what its intentions are: these have been
real problems. Linked to that is the problem of governance:
who does make decisions about this program or any other
program? We're trying to move into a very participatory
kind of situation. In that sense, a hierarchy provides clarity;
and participatory kinds of decision-making make things
very fuzzy. The difficulty is getting people to really take responsibility for governing themselves even though in the
meantime they don't want you to tell them what to do.*

Another leader of a similar institution spoke more favorably
about planning and of the need for time to do it: "I requested
eighteen months after the entire faculty had been hired in order to
plan and have time for experimentation. I was laughed at by University staff members, by members of the board. It was just considered insane that anything like that could be supported. After everything went haywire in the first year with students and a lot of things
had taken place, we then had the astute observation from University
staff members that the college shouldn't have opened when it did.
I think the pattern is that we have a couple of hundred years developing a tradition and then we're presumptuous enough to try to
turn the whole thing around in a year and expect everyone to
function on a completely different basis. If you express it, you get
all sorts of denials that anybody expects that of you, but in fact
they do."

Specific Problems

As these lengthy quotations suggest, the problems which confront program designers, either before they begin operations or
later, appear in complex, interlocked forms which give rise to a
feeling of stress. No issue can be separated from the others without
holding constant all other matters which are, in practice, always in
a state of flux; but such separation is essential if each issue is to be
considered on its own terms.

For what clientele is the program to be planned? The leaders of every external-degree program need to begin by considering
this question. The sponsoring institution is influenced in its choice
by its tradition (unless a new college is to be created), its aims and
aspirations, its resources, its geographic location, its established clientele patterns, and its access to key leaders who can help achieve its
desires once they are defined. In many cases, the only possible clientele is students already enrolled; the immediate community or the
constituency offers no other students, particularly among adults. But
the influence of creative leadership in finding clienteles cannot be
ignored. Neither Plainfield, Vermont, nor Norman, Oklahoma,
seem likely places to initiate external degrees for adults; Yellow
Springs, Ohio, is an unexpected spot for the center of a national
multipurpose institution. Yet all three locations are conducting successful external-degree efforts.

Three basic clienteles for adult programs are suggested at
the end of Chapter Three: those who ordinarily would have gone
to college in youth but didn't; a meritocratic elite; the disadvantaged. The first clientele is probably the most numerous and widespread, and there is some evidence that programs planned for either
the second or the third group attract many students belonging to
the first; certainly this has been true of the Open University in
Great Britain.

These three clienteles are, in fact, clusterings of audiences.
The actual nature of the proposed clientele is determined by the
people available. For example, an external-degree program is seldom planned simply for "the disadvantaged"; it is created to serve
a special racial, ethnic, or sexual group living in a specific geographic neighborhood and showing distinct needs for counseling,

admission, teaching, and evaluation. Examples of this approach are to be found in many community colleges today; Cross explores the needs of segments of this audience in her book *Beyond the Open Door.*

The same specificity applies in the other two clienteles. The Master of Liberal Arts program at Johns Hopkins University, for example, was created after long planning to provide an integrated program in the history of ideas for people who had already established themselves in the learned professions or otherwise distinguished themselves. Of the students enrolled in one year, "forty-four had more than one baccalaureate degree, fifty-three had master's degrees, and nine had earned doctoral degrees."[3] In the first three years of the program (1962–1965), 480 such people enrolled, most from Baltimore but some from other cities and states. Of these people, only forty-six withdrew, most because of changes in their personal lives.

Even within the category of "second-chance" students, careful attention must be given to the identification of a special audience. The president of a woman's college in a large city tells how this was done in her institution:

We found that many women who wished to return to college were frustrated. One, by the fact that because many of their credits were old, they were not accepted by many institutions. Two, many established institutions, particularly state universities, were not willing to accept part-time women. Three, the age level. Many schools were not willing to accept women over thirty-five. And fourthly, the time in which courses were planned was very often late in the evening, the time when husbands and children are home. Growing out of this situation came our plan. One, to try to provide classes that were flexible for the person who had to have babysitting, for instance, to come once a week for a seminar. Certain courses can be taught that way, others can't. Two, when they returned initially, they would be with women their own age until they got adjusted and

[3] This information, like the other data here cited, is drawn from brochures made available by the University.

then moved into the regular curriculum. Many women would do this by the second year and some would take two years. Three, age was no obstacle. We have them as old as sixty-five and as young as twenty-eight. They would have to be full-time students for one year before we would admit them to credit by examination. Credit by examination was unlimited in the number of credits they could obtain provided the chairman of the department concerned was willing to accept the credit. This has primarily been successful in art, language, literature, and drama. It has rarely been used to any great extent in anything like math or science.

In most situations, the actual clientele reached will not be exactly the one defined in advance. Sometimes unexpected students can be absorbed with little difficulty. For example, the program just described now includes another category of "second-chance" students, men whose working day permits them to fit the classes into their schedule. When a wholly different type of clientele appears, however, serious problems are likely to arise. As one program director put it, "There are profoundly different implications as to the format when you are talking about an under-twenty-three or an over-twenty-three group. That would also be true in terms of defining constituencies—minority, third-world, disadvantaged. You have to be terribly self-conscious about whom you are trying to reach."

Some institutions insist upon serving everyone. One director said that his program had been built upon the desire to serve everyone adolescent or older, regardless of background, and to include "people without high school diplomas, college drop-outs, creative people with different lifestyles, also adults and minority and low-income people." (It is worth noting that—in the second of the three long quotations near the start of this chapter—it was this director who indicated a strong sense of frustration when asked about the major problems of his program.) Universities adopting this approach for political or other reasons usually find that they must establish special ways for coping with the resulting problems: creating a cluster of programs rather than one; developing strong counseling and guidance centers; or selecting a diverse teaching staff whose members are able to work on an individualized basis.

What is the essential meaning of the degree to be designed? Since current thought about external degrees centers on the baccalaureate, it will be the focus of attention here. As the term *baccalaureate* is currently used in the United States, it appears to have four overlapping meanings.

(1) It signifies the accomplishment of four years of residential study, nine months a year, beyond the secondary school. During these four years, the student acquires about 125 semester-hours of credit (or their equivalent in some other standardized measuring system) which fit into an accepted pattern of concentration and distribution of subject matter. To secure these credits, the student must perform at an acceptable level of quality, one representing the average performance in the classes which he attends. The course of study may be closely prescribed, or the student may have the freedom to choose implied by the observation of an Archbishop of Canterbury that "a university is a place where a multitude of studies are conducted with no relation between them except that of simultaneity and juxtaposition."

(2) It signifies the mastery of a body of knowledge of a serious and intricate sort; this is the classic conception of the degree. At the Oxford of 1250 or the Yale of 1850, the student was expected to study certain traditional books which conveyed the essential ideas of man's culture as it had been laboriously developed since ancient times. Some colleges today, particularly those with dominant occupational or religious orientations, still hold to this conviction.

(3) It signifies that the recipient has become a different sort of person—as defined either by tradition or by the faculty of the institution—from the one who entered the college. The classic college attempted to develop the potential of the student's mind, character, and body; to create a "whole" man or woman, disciplined to serve as a competent citizen and an able controller of personal concerns. A liberal education gives mankind the power and, therefore, the freedom to act. Today this conception has been supplemented and, in many cases, replaced by defining competence either as the capacity to do certain specific things well or as successful preparation for advanced training which will further refine certain specialized capacities.

(4) It signifies the completion of a process of acculturation, the molding of an individual by his residence on or near a campus and by his interaction with faculty members and other students. In this process, childhood is replaced by adulthood. This acculturation may be of a general or a special sort. Employers have long restricted certain kinds of positions or given pay differentials to individuals holding the baccalaureate on the grounds either that it demonstrated certain specific accomplishments or that it certified that its possessor was broader in outlook or of a superior capacity to one who did not have the degree.

In this fourth sense, each college has an ethos which distinguishes it from all others. In the earlier, more restricted days of higher education, the Harvard aesthete, the Yale athlete, and the University of Virginia aristocrat were accepted, though perhaps never seriously, as distinctive types. Modern social psychology has taken up this theme in great depth, and colleges today are treated by many investigators (both intuitive analysts and developers of objective instruments measuring psychological press) as social organisms, each with its own distinctive way of life. This view so pervades the serious literature of higher education today that both scholars and laymen take it virtually for granted.[4] Once a college ethos has emerged, it perpetuates itself. The degrees conferred by such institutions, however much they mechanically resemble those of other institutions, have distinctive overtones which are evident to the perceptive observer.

While these four meanings are general in nature and may overlap each other, each acquires its own proponents; the differences among them run deep and often serve as visible or hidden barriers to communication in a discussion of the external degree. Any administrative or faculty group designing a new program must consider, throughout its deliberations, which meaning of the degree it considers dominant.

If the first is adopted, the external degree becomes a matter of establishing a traditional program at times or places available to

[4] A summary of research on the topic can be found in G. G. Stern, *People in Context* (New York: Wiley, 1970). A series of case studies is presented by M. Keeton and C. Hilberry, *Struggle and Promise* (New York: McGraw-Hill, 1969).

the student who cannot undertake the internal degree. Alternatively, the task is one of identifying equivalents for courses by subject-matter tests, examinations in fields of content, directed work experience, or by other means. Often the nature of the teaching is changed for the new audience which is to be instructed; thus learning may be accomplished by television, supervised independent study, work projects, intensive residential study, or by other means.

If the second or the third meanings of the baccalaureate are adopted, the planning for the external degree rests essentially on the nature of the final assessment. The question to be answered is either "has the person concerned mastered the accepted body of knowledge?" or "is he or she the kind of person who should possess the bachelor's degree?" The first is easier to cope with than the second, since the latter signifies qualities of mind, behavior, and character difficult to measure.

If the fourth meaning is adopted, the external degree is defined by the establishment of a new kind of acculturation. The form traditionally provided by residence on a campus is ruled out, and its place must be taken by the new means chosen. One new university established itself to grant the fourth type of baccalaureate and defined the key elements of the acculturation it hoped to achieve, one of them being a strong commitment to urban life. Therefore, it will certify only students who can and will live good and effective lives in the city. In the words of its chief administrator: "We wouldn't be neutral about the city and we sure as hell wouldn't be anti-city: we'd be pro-city." To achieve this, the student is acculturated to the city by saturation in its life and works. It serves the place for him that the dormitory, dining hall, classroom, athletic facilities, and informal college life do for the internal-degree student.

How compatible with customary academic procedures should external-degree requirements be? Should external-degree requirements be stated in terms of credits, honor points, recognized majors and minors, established patterns of specialization and distribution, grades, residence requirements, and all the other procedures of American academic life in the last hundred years? Or should the new degrees ignore standard arrangements and start afresh? No sharper practical issue confronts the designer and administrators of the external degree.

The issue is related to the goal of the program but (as will be demonstrated) is exacerbated by the special needs of students who are in constant motion—geographically, institutionally, and in terms of their personal desires and ambitions. Sharp, clear contrasts in viewpoint are evident in the answers to this question. One young administrator of a non-traditional external-degree program observed decisively: "As far as curricular compatibility is concerned, I think that if a project is worth doing from the standpoint of the clientele you want to serve, you ought to go ahead and not concern yourself with compatibility. If you're involved in something non-traditional, you can't hope at the outset at least to dovetail with traditional programs." Another young administrator was equally decisive on the other side: "It's absolutely essential that the offerings in a non-traditional program be, in some sense, directly convertible into standard credit hours. Our major drop-out problem is not due to ability, but to job transfer. We lose 18–20 percent of our students because they move or change jobs. The program has to be real credit or they're going to be disillusioned, usually for the second or third time in their lives, and probably won't go back."

The planners of adult and assessment degrees are caught in a real dilemma. On one hand, they wish to be creative in rethinking the ends and means of a college education and in designing wholly new programs. If they move too far in this direction, however, they isolate their students from the mainstream of past and present education. Academic credit already earned cannot be used in the new program, and if students want to convert later to other programs they may have a hard time securing recognition for what they have learned. On the other hand, if the planners of a new program rigorously follow current patterns of internal-degree requirements so that credit can be easily converted, the advantages of innovation and creativity in both ends and means are lost; students in the program wind up with routines established for other kinds of students in other places.

Both extremes now exist. Some new degree programs (both adult and assessment) differ essentially from the typical patterns of American higher education and therefore can neither offer advanced standing on the basis of credits earned previously nor provide their students with any method of transferring work completed in the program. The extension degree, however, offers a regular program at a different time or place; its students can transfer in and out at will. But the program offered does not consider their maturity of viewpoint, make use of what they have learned from experience and informal study, nor take advantage of their special lifestyles.

The effort to strike a middle position, to achieve compatibility while maintaining creativity in curriculum or method, has led some program designers to adopt varied strategies. The simplest has been to retain the concept of formal credit and other traditional-degree elements but to permit their achievement by such devices as CLEP, other examinations, or by the fulfillment of contracts.

Other programs use other devices, the most common of which is to establish a table converting the units appropriate to the novel curricular design to semester-hour or other traditional credit measurements. "We've been able," said one director, "to get along internally very well without any kind of a semester-hour system—through the use of behavioral objectives and insistence on a demonstration of mastery as a means of graduating students. But [since we have] to join the mainstream, . . . I have a data system currently being developed which will provide a transcript." Another director said, "The students ask about what's being put on their transcripts: we have now equated these units into equivalent credit hours." Sometimes the establishment of equivalence can be carried to startling lengths. One nationally known and highly esteemed president said bluntly: "What we do in our most radical program . . . is give sixteen credits of liberal arts for nothing. What the registrar's office does, though, is prorate these units across the various disciplines."

Another device is to suggest to students that they clear their prospective programs in advance with the upper-divisional or graduate schools which they plan to enter later. Other students wait to make a case for their earlier work when they apply to these schools. Sometimes they succeed. For example, the president just quoted observed: "Many transfer institutions will give credit without looking for one-to-one correspondence. They'll give us credit for English 1, social science 1, and psychology 1, even though they can't recognize anything in our program that looks like those."

It is likely, however, that many students have substantial difficulties when they confront the advanced schools. Such problems can arise even when the student seeks to enter a non-traditional college or university. The president of one such upper-division institution remarked ruefully that "we are having problems, as many schools are, with students who are exerting pressure on us to give them credit for experience."

How should the new program be financed? The question of financing includes a host of issues with relatively few answers, because few objective studies have been conducted. Existing studies often do not take account of crucial aspects of costing, even such obvious factors as overhead institutional expenses, marginal costs of otherwise unused facilities, foregone earnings of students, hidden subsidies provided by underpaid teachers, maintenance of supporting services (such as counseling, libraries, health-care centers, and student-meeting facilities), and differences in part-time and full-time fees. As yet, the possible economies of the new methods of instruction have not been tested because, with few exceptions, they have been used only as supplements to conventional approaches. Lawrence P. Grayson points out that "the concept of a teacher supervising thirty students, each of whom is seated at a computer terminal performing drill and practice exercises, is a costly use of the technology. This approach does not reduce the student-teacher ratio or make instruction available to the student at his convenience or in different locations. The potential of technology for individualizing and personalizing instruction and for allowing more effective instructional patterns can only be realized with organizational change."[5]

As institutional leaders consider whether they wish to embark on an external degree program, only a few financial guidelines are available, some of them ambiguous.

(1) The extension degree and the administrative unit which supports it and other educational services tend to produce revenue for their universities. In at least a few cases, they are maintained precisely because they help support other parts of the institution.

---

[5] L. P. Grayson, "Cost, Benefits, Effectiveness: Challenge to Educational Technology." *Science,* March 17, 1972, *175,* 1222.

One dean of an evening college points out that his is "presently the only solvent unit of the University" even though it pays "almost a million dollars just [to keep] the administration going." Cost studies have been made, and funds provided by his college are allocated to other parts of the institution; 45 percent of the cost of the registrar's office and 20 percent of the cost of the library are paid by these funds. The size of the operation gives the college sufficient margin to undertake new and bold endeavors; among other offerings it has a successful external master's degree designed especially for adults. This institution is nationally known as one of the best-administered adult-education units in the country. Its example indicates what can be done by prudent and careful leadership operating in a relatively favorable setting, though with no general financial support from government.

(2) Some special degrees for adults are less expensive than internal degrees at the same university; some are more costly. The director of one adult degree program asserts that "we are economically productive to the college" but hedges a bit by saying that "we're just now going to do some very careful cost accounting." On the other hand, Bailey has noted that "experience with Syracuse University's external degree in liberal studies over six years suggests that students get a better education than on campus, but that the off-campus program is more expensive."[6] But even directors of external degrees who argue that their programs are less costly than internal degrees think that the situation may change in the future and that prudent management is essential if costs are to be kept down. One administrator put the matter this way:

This is a small and in some senses a poor university. Because of this, budgets for a program follow development rather than anticipate the development. You are given a little money to get something running, and as student enrollment grows more money is given.

Right now it costs less to educate my students, and the reason is because of the part-time faculty. The pay is much lower, there is no overhead and no question of ten-

[6] Bailey, p. 175.

ure. Within the next six to eight years, however, our people are likely to cost close to what some of the others do. There is much less baggage in this college. There are no load reductions. With the part-time instructors, I can break even with six students to a section, and, as I'm running 17.5 people per section, you can see that the profit margin is quite large. But I think this is temporary. I think since we are new and are growing up in an era in which you watch your pennies, we are going to be able to keep our cost pretty much in line in that we can anticipate a lot of problems that weren't anticipated twenty years ago in the other colleges.

(3) A great deal of attention must be given in cost accounting to the maintenance of quality. A pioneering program centered on independent, self-directed study must figure its instructional costs differently than one based on the number of contact hours between teacher and students in the classroom. If the heart of the program lies in close supervision by a mentor, sometimes one who must use expensive equipment, the cost of this one-to-one relationship will be higher than that for a one-to-ten or one-to-thirty classroom unit. Furthermore, all auxiliary services—library, laboratory, counseling, and other learning facilities—must be calculated in terms of quality as the program defines it, not by the generalized indices used for conventional activities.

(4) None of the major non-traditional assessment-degree programs in the United States have existed long enough to demonstrate their ongoing financial viability. Their start-up costs came from government or foundations, and there has not been time for student fees or other sources of income to provide a secure ongoing income. Claims that external degrees are less expensive than internal degrees have been made and have had some political impact. In both England and the United States, some conservatives believe that since it apparently has become necessary to give the masses the educational opportunity they desire, it is best to do so in situations not requiring heavy capital outlay and tenured faculty members. If the cost differential between internal and external instruction turns out to be inconsequential, or if the external degree becomes

more expensive than the internal degree, political battles over cost are unavoidable.

(5) If the external-degree program is to be experimental, new systems must be devised for assessing student fees. The usual patterns of support for higher education are from taxes, endowment income, tuition fees, financial contributions, special fees for service (such as those from hospital patients), funds given by donors for specific projects, and the contributed service of ill-paid or nonpaid faculty members. Tuition income is directly related to course-taking, and other forms of income for instruction are indirectly related to it. (The funds provided by legislatures often are granted by a formula based on cost per pupil or on faculty-load requirements.)

The external degree may alter this pattern radically. The evening college offering an extension degree may have a lower tuition charge than that assessed on campus—usually because the market will not bear higher cost. Savings are made because of a heavier student load, a lower-paid faculty, and the failure to provide adequate libraries, counseling, audiovisual centers, or other auxiliary services. How to assess charges for non-traditional programs not based on the accumulation of standard credits but on such methods as independent study, tutorial teaching, instruction by television, short courses and conferences, intensive counseling, and comprehensive examinations is a serious question. Directors of such programs must either develop new bases for tuition fees or construct elaborate tables of conversion to traditional credit-hour charges. Some public institutions are handicapped in their choice because of legislative requirements concerning fees. One state, for example, requires that a student activity fee be charged. For internal-degree students, the charge is $15 a quarter; for external-degree students, a one-time charge of $1 is made, but the law has been followed to the letter.

(6) The out-of-pocket costs to both student and university usually are much less for the external degree than for the internal degree. The student need not make duplicate housing and eating arrangements, his travel costs may be diminished, and he may not have to forego so much of his earnings. It is true, however, that he may suffer penalties which offset these gains, for fellowships and

other grants are less common for part-time than for full-time students. But the net difference in immediate cost may be sufficient to permit him to attend college, a privilege he would otherwise be denied.

For the college or university (particularly one experiencing a decline in number of internal students), the chief cost benefit of an external degree program comes from more efficient use of its human and building resources. Fixed costs, such as heat, light, and maintenance, can be spread over a larger number of students. Specialized faculty members may be maintained whom the university would otherwise not have enough students to support. Some teaching may be done part-time by community people whom the university could not hope to attract on a full-time basis and to whom it need not pay full-time salaries. To the hard-pressed administrator, these savings may be important in dealing with immediate necessities.

The savings may be more apparent than real, however; some economists and cost accountants warn that in the long run external-degree programs may prove more expensive than internal degree programs if quality of instruction is to be maintained. As already noted, many of the new methods of instruction are more expensive than the old ones. Some faculty members reject the new ways but remain securely in their tenured positions, and some physical facilities cannot be used but must be maintained. It might be more effective and economical to remedy a decline in internal students by vigorous promotional campaigns than to make commitments to students demanding services the institution is not designed to give. In fact, it might be better to retrench, reduce the size of the institution, and maintain a lean, flexible, and effective traditional service.

Such matters ultimately rest on the situation faced by each institution. It must make careful calculations and projections as to what the future holds for it. If it offers an external degree, it must be prepared, in subsequent years, to change its figures in light of experience. And it must always calculate and recalculate the financial influence of new program on existing ones. Will the external degree harm or aid the survival of the internal degree? In individual cases, either result is possible.

In national terms, the issue is not one of immediate cost but of ultimate gain. Even if the addition of the external degree requires funds which otherwise would not be spent, it provides a substantial education to countless students who would not secure it otherwise. Leaving aside (but only for a moment) all the personal satisfactions and rewards which come from the possession of a degree, its provision by society is a capital investment which will return substantial dividends both to the individual and to the society. If external degrees enable those who otherwise would be denied an education to receive it, the eventual cost of *not* providing such degrees is greater than the cost of having them.

How great is the interest in an external degree? The interest of potential students in the external degree is considered on a national basis in Chapter Three, but institutional decisions must be local and vary greatly from place to place. Statistics may show a sizable population base with potential interest in an external degree at a specific college, yet such figures must be treated with caution. Many people are fortunate to have gotten as far as they did; they neither want nor can profit from more education. Others have so low a desire for learning that they will not make substantial contributions in time or money to secure it. Some do not have the economic resources to invest in themselves, however much they might like to do so. Finally, many people, for a variety of reasons, are simply not good risks for further education, and any sensible counselor would urge them not to undertake it.

It may also be true that the mere announcement of a program will bring forth those needed to fill it. One director observed, "There seems to be such a pool of students in this city and surrounding areas that are interested in this kind of program that I really have trouble, with my limited staff, keeping up with the students who simply walk in the door. I've got over one thousand students registered, and I literally begged the admissions office to lay off any advertising." Another optimistic statement came from the director in a more sparsely settled area: "The problem is trying to serve all the students that want to be served. We have a number of people in a 'holding pattern,' ready to go as soon as we can serve them. We want to move slowly, to establish an economic base, so that when we take on a program or serve a group of people we can do all the things that we say we can in the brochure."

The picture is not always so rosy. Another director serving a substantial population base but administering a rigorous program ("we're dealing with a select clientele: we don't see ourselves as doing all things for all people") has talked "in some way or other" with about forty-five hundred people but has enrolled only about 112. He believes that the solution to his enrollment problem is highly selective and intensive advertising.

These figures suggest one of the most important elements about external degrees, particularly those designed for adults. Although mentioned previously, it deserves repetition in the present context. Men and women cannot undertake an external degree program in the abstract. They can only choose or reject specific proposals presented as concrete realities. Until recently, educators have worked in a relatively stable and protected market in which eighteen- to twenty-two-year olds go on to college, fulfilling the expectations of society and coming from homes in which educational expenditures take first priority. With the external degree, however, the institution confronts a more volatile market. It must design a program which can be fitted into life patterns not built around education and must present and conduct that program to compete successfully against conflicting demands on time and economic resources. More subtly, the underlying social expectation is that young people will go to college if they can, whereas it is taken for granted that adults will not. Therefore, the adult student must reject the beliefs of those around him. Research demonstrates that many adults feel a widespread antagonism to study expressed by those closest to them: their husbands or wives, their best friends, their parents, or their children.

It is not wise, therefore, for an institution to move into an external degree program until it has made careful probes to discover whether there is a potential clientele available which will respond to the design it presents.

Who should take the initiative in advocating and administering an external degree? The simplest response to this question is "whoever feels the need," but that answer is probably too general to satisfy anybody. The history of the extension degree is not sufficiently rich to indicate who, on the whole, proposed it. Presumably some were created by presidents and other administrators, while others grew out of the activities of extension divisions, which have administered most, though not all, of them. Special degrees for adults were largely the creation of a few deans of extension divisions, sometimes initially assisted by foundation grants and sometimes responding to the pressures (and the contracts)' of various branches of the armed services eager to develop an officer corps whose members had college degrees. These early efforts, supported by new systems of measurement created chiefly by the Educational Testing Service and the College Entrance Examination Board, created the climate for the growth of assessment degrees in the 1970s. And certainly the sustained and imaginative interest of the Carnegie Corporation throughout the post–World War II years has had a marked influence, as has (more recently) the Ford Foundation and other sources of funds.

In the first three years of the 1970s, however, the impetus toward bold new programs has come from major academic and political figures: chancellors, presidents, governors, leaders of the legislature, and commissioners of education. (Educational folklore has it that one governor announced a new statewide external-degree program on the spur of the moment simply because he did not have anything else to say at a scheduled press conference.) Academic senates have been involved in decision-making but usually only after the matter was referred to them by the president—though it is possible that adroit faculty maneuvering sometimes may have stimulated that referral. In general, however, it appears that the new emphasis on the external degree started at the top of the policy-making and administrative structure and filtered down, to some extent catching extension workers by surprise; such is a key idea in the presidential address of Floyd B. Fischer at the 1972 meeting of the National University Extension Association.[7]

This conviction is borne out by the supply study mentioned in the Preface. Within the context of a general inquiry into uncon-

[7] F. B. Fischer, "Uneasiness in an Era of Romance." *The Spectator,* June 1972, *36,* 8.

ventional study, American institutions of higher learning were asked
to identify "the *one undergraduate program* that seems likely to receive the greatest resources and support at your institution in the
near future." Of the 351 programs thus identified, 63 percent involved the awarding of degrees. These 63 percent were not analyzed
separately but, of the total number of 351, 20 percent were administered by an officer of the central administration (some of whom
may have had a special responsibility for extension), 42 percent by
a general academic dean, 18 percent by a separate extension office,
2 percent by a separate special organization, and 11 percent by some
other officer or committee; no information was collected on 6 percent. Since most of these programs were relatively new (about two-
thirds of them were less than three years old), their ultimate dispo-
sition in the university or college hierarchy remains uncertain, but
it seems clear that their point of origin was at or near the top of the
authority structure. This fact may facilitate the transfer of lessons
learned in the external degree program to the practices used in the
internal degree.

The figures indicate that external degrees presently are not
administered chiefly by extension divisions. The heads of such divisions vary markedly in their viewpoint on that fact. Presumably
almost all would like this responsibility; and some feel that if extension units (including evening colleges) do not operate the program,
the university should not maintain it. Others agree with Robert F.
Ray, dean of Extension at the University of Iowa: "The important
thing is to get the job done, and where extension divisions aren't
prepared to do the job then indeed there ought to be new structures."[8] Still another view is that expressed by Floyd B. Fischer,
dean of the Extension Division at Pennsylvania State University:
that the true function of such a division is to be the center of programs for part-time students, whether they be in degree-awarding
or degree-free programs; and that, in remaining true to this function, "we will continue to be traditional and non-traditional. We
will continue to be imaginative and adaptive, using testing and
counseling and presenting instruction through many modes,"[9] never

[8] Quoted in *The Chronicle of Higher Education,* May 22, 1972, *6,* 2.
[9] Fischer, p. 8.

letting the external degree become the sole or even the central focus of attention.

How can faculty support be won for the program? Most administrators who have initiated external-degree programs indicate that, in one way or another, the securing of positive and continuing collaboration by the faculty is indispensable to change. Institutions of higher learning have two internal systems of power, the administrative and the academic; and ever since the beginning of the academic guilds which created the medieval university, the faculty has had rights of policy-making which could effectively change or checkmate the plans of presidents and deans. The amount of control and the way it is exercised vary from one institution to another, but the collective decision-making processes of individuals (each of whom has a highly specialized competence) are a complex matter. In the early 1900s, Josiah Royce, a professor of philosophy at Harvard, commented, "I have no difficulty with Hegel's Absolute; that is simple. What I cannot follow are the discussions at the faculty meetings."[10] Royce was not the last person to find them baffling.

Every creator of an external degree in an existing institution recognizes, however, that his program must have champions in the academic community and that the new plans must be approved by the controlling boards of the faculty and usually by the senate itself. One dean said, "It's important to get senior faculty involved and participating to meet *your own* purposes—not to meet *their* purposes," and his strategy for doing so is based on personal contact and persuasion. But faculty senates can be contentious, resisting the blandishments of even the most persuasive deans. The director of one adult degree program reported that it was approved by the major policy-making body only over strongly voiced opposition, and that "a good deal of bitterness carries through to today, six years later. Presenting specific and empirical evidence doesn't seem to shake this vague uneasiness. The fact that our people perform as well as and often better than the regular students in Arts and Sciences doesn't seem to shake these people from their assertions that

[10] *Abraham Flexner: An Autobiography* (New York: Simon and Schuster, 1960), p. 64.

our students are not first-rate." Another administrator, this one a
president, put the matter succinctly: "The biggest problem we're
having right now is faculty backlash."

A much happier outcome was reported by the director of
another program: "Looking at starting a program, I think the biggest major problem is getting your faculty involved: getting them
to develop some confidence in this method of offering a degree and
then eventually winning them to the point where they support it
and then eventually become enthusiastic about it. I think we can
honestly say that here, faculty members who want to teach in this
program have to knock on the door now, because it's considered a
very prestigious program. But four years ago, faculty were looking
at us as sort of a maverick operation that was going to downgrade
the degree." When asked how this had been brought about, he answered that it had been accomplished by the innate quality of the
program and the caliber of the students. Why this fact had been
true for him but not for the previously quoted dean is not clear.

To one academic vice-president, the strategy for winning
faculty assent for an external degree was one of gradualism—the
movement of an initially peripheral activity toward the center of the
institution:

> In the area of integrating the external-degree pro-
> gram with on-campus programs, we had some special prob-
> lems, some of which we've solved and some we're still work-
> ing on. There is always the problem of academic credibility
> —and it has been the primary problem. We approached it
> in several ways: First of all, we said that this program had
> to be more academically sound and stronger than ongoing
> programs because it's going to have to stand up against
> more careful scrutiny. So we began to develop procedures
> whereby we could hopefully insure that kind of credibility.
> This meant getting our faculty very much involved, with
> the faculty essentially making primary policy decisions and
> some of the routine decisions. We were also concerned about
> getting our procedures integrated through our regular re-
> cording system and our regular graduation procedures, and
> so forth. We began by developing a program that was quite

independent as far as administrative details were concerned, and we kept it on a separate track from what the ongoing programs of our graduate school office, our records office, our admissions office were doing. (We did stay with our regular admissions requirements, however.) Then after we got it operating with a few courses, we began a process of integrating these procedures into our regular procedures. So we are bringing it into the fold, although it didn't start that way. With a program such as ours, we needed to develop it independently at first. We wanted to save that innovative aspect of it, and to get something ready first. But we didn't allow it to get so far afield that we couldn't get it integrated. We kept it separate for a time because that seemed to give us the most flexibility in dealing with the program.

Can faculty members carry out the unusual requirements imposed by the external degree? In the 351 special programs analyzed in the supply study (about two-thirds of which are degree programs), no information is available on the faculty composition of 5 percent of the institutions. In the others, however, the distribution of faculty members is as shown in Table 13.

The mix of these four kinds of faculty varies greatly from

Table 13

FACULTY DISTRIBUTION IN EXTERNAL-DEGREE PROGRAMS

	Majority	*Minority*	*None*
		Percent	
Regular faculty also teaching conventional programs	62	17	16
Separate faculty chosen for the program	13	18	64
Special instructors from the community	16	39	40
Others (graduate students, retired faculty)	4	3	89

one institution to another, as does a mix divided on any other basis. The director of such a program, therefore, must confront the issue of faculty competence in a complex fashion; and the selection, training, and disengagement of faculty members is likely to cause him more problems than any other of his responsibilities, particularly if the external degree is sponsored by an institution offering an internal degree as well and using its "regular" faculty to teach in the unconventional programs (as appears to be the case in the institutions reported in Table 13). It is the attempt to use that faculty effectively which has led, both here and abroad, to the creation of new institutions for external degrees by people who despair of the ability of the faculty members of existing colleges and universities to adjust to the new demands made upon them.

Many who ask if faculty can carry out the demands imposed by the external degree have in mind a stereotypical faculty member who drones on to a captive audience of restless young people and who could never capture the minds and imaginations of students in external-degree programs. While such professors do, in fact, serve on the teaching staffs of American colleges and universities, they are not necessarily the majority or even the mode. Faculty members vary greatly in their capacity to adapt to new audiences, new methods, and new formulations of content. Many already work successfully with groups of adult students either as part of their university duties or independently, and there is no apparent reason why they could not serve in and would not welcome an external-degree program which would offer them a unique challenge. Furthermore, if the program employed unfamiliar methods of teaching, many faculty members would recognize the need for special training in their use. Thus the direct answer to the question is "some can and some can't."

The reference in the previous paragraph to "special training" suggests that opportunities for it must be provided both on separate campuses and in regional or national courses or workshops. Faculty members learned (at least to some degree) how to lecture, discuss, give demonstrations, or make library assignments from their own education and from observing the processes of their colleagues. But non-traditional techniques present a new challenge. Where is a professor to learn to guide an independent learner, evaluate a contract, recommend noncampus instructional resources, assess the educative effect of experience, use new techniques of communication, create learning modules, or perform any of the tasks which may be required by the external degree? The most efficient way of conveying these skills and understandings is by training opportunities in which institutional programs may be facilitated and also in which professors from different campuses can share their experiences and refine their ways of work.

One question of importance to the faculty is: will the system of academic promotions and reinforcements be modified to reward those who teach in external-degree programs? At present the system works heavily in favor of the internal degree. Both administrators and colleagues tend to favor the "regular" faculty member, the one who meets his classes on campus, is present to perform his committee duties, and makes up a part of the network of informal communication which is so important in college and university life. The teacher at night; the lecturer whose class is far from campus; the professor on television; the counselor, mentor, or tutor; or the person who relates chiefly to nonorthodox students appears outside the accepted establishment. Therefore any university which undertakes an external-degree program must try to reward its faculty members adequately and help them to become a continuing part of the community of scholars.

Some people are temperamentally unable to stand the openness of unconventional programs, and it is often hard to predict how individuals will be affected. One president pungently noted, "It's surprising that people who appear to be academic radicals in conventional settings can be rather dramatically unnerved when they are put in a setting where they are no longer radicals." This point was generalized and further developed by the president of another institution, who said:

> *The major problem that I would see is that the time required for planning, the specific activities that constitute the planning, and the emotional demands that are made on the individuals who are asked to work in a way which is completely unfamiliar to all of them is underestimated. There are good people who just cannot function in situa-*

tions where there is no structure. And much as they may talk about freedom and liberty and flexibility and all that, the minute they're left free to structure the world any way they want to structure it, they're paralyzed. There should be a graceful manner of exit for any administrator, faculty, or staff member who can't meet it emotionally to be allowed to continue what may have been an outstanding career along traditional forms, so it shouldn't bother them. The personal strain of trying to move where no one else has gone before can be much more demanding than anyone has acknowledged. One of the reasons for going back to familiar patterns is that they don't have all of this stress and strain attached to them.

Conclusion

The questions raised in this chapter are so daunting and so resistant to simple answers that they must give pause to the leaders of every institution contemplating the introduction of an external degree. But, as Chapter Three shows, the need is great; and instruments are being forged by which that need can be met. The chief requirement is the resolute determination that the task must be accomplished. "You've got to have a strong, articulate, hard leadership at the top," says the strong, articulate, hard leader of one program. "We know around here that our whole professional lives are at stake—that if this thing falls on its face there isn't going to be any second chance for any of us."

Nothing is ever created and perfected at the same moment—and so it will be with the external degree as it moves into the third phase of its development in the United States. "We shall make some mistakes," said one program director, "we shall enroll some people we should not enroll and doubtless we shall award some degrees we should not award. And so," he concluded, "we shall be admitted to the great brotherhood of higher education."

6

Problems of
General Policy

If a new idea were to be admitted only when it had definitely proved its justification or even if we merely demanded that it must have a clear and definite meaning at the outset, then such a demand might gravely hamper the progress of science. We must never forget that ideas devoid of a clear meaning frequently gave the strongest impulse to the further development of science. The idea . . . of perpetual motion gave rise to an intelligent comprehension of energy; the idea of the absolute velocity of the earth gave rise to the theory of relativity; and the idea that the electronic movement resembled that of the planets was the origin of atomic physics. These are indisputable facts, and they give rise to thought, for they show clearly that in science as elsewhere fortune favors the brave.

MAX PLANCK

147

*T*he American educator who visits almost any foreign nation soon realizes that, unlike his own country, it has an organized system of higher education, one which may be diverse in form and lacking in symmetry but nonetheless possesses pattern and shape. In some countries, the external degree offers a way of protecting the established order and is accepted at least in part because it opens the door to opportunity for those who want to learn while diminishing demands which might lead to expensive or disruptive changes in the traditional educational system.

In the United States, higher education has grown from many different origins; nothing resembling a formal system exists. Yet diversity of control and purpose has not kept institutions from uniformities of practice, many adopted by a process of unreasoned imitation but now so strengthened by tradition that they are seldom questioned. The proposal of the assessment degree by some of the most prestigious centers of educational thought in the United States, therefore, gives rise to many issues of educational policy, some at the heart of American practice. These issues influence the leaders of institutions proposing the assessment degree and are, therefore, an extension of the issues mentioned in Chapter Five but are treated here as evidences of national concern rather than in institutional terms.

Why do people want an external degree? The simplest answer, and perhaps the best, is: for all the reasons they want an internal degree. But an element has been added by the nature of the current audience because most people who seek an external degree today are adults who interrupted the "normal course" of their education but now wish to resume it. The reasons given for external study are numerous and complex, belying the implication that getting or keeping a job is the only feasible reason for further study. In the most advanced research now available, Paul Burgess uses cluster analysis to discern the basic reasons for participation given by a large sample of adult students engaged in many fields of study. He concludes that seven basic factors can be identified: the desire to know, the desire to reach a personal goal, the desire to reach a social goal, the desire to reach a religious goal, the desire to take part in social activity, the desire to escape, and the desire to meet formal requirements.[1] (In his study, these factors are analyzed in depth and are harmonized with the findings of other studies.)

Using the general framework developed by Burgess, an as-yet-unpublished study of the learning motives of a national strati-fied sample of people age eighteen to sixty not in full-time atten-dance at any school was made in midsummer 1972.[2] A first question defined "would-be learners" by asking, "Is there anything in par-ticular that you'd like to know more about, or would like to learn how to do better?" To this question, 76.77 percent responded in the affirmative. If this figure is projected to the whole population, it would indicate that about 79.8 million people in the country are would-be learners. Respondents were also asked, "Within the past twelve months, have you received (or are you receiving) instruction in *any* of the following subjects or skills?" A long list of topics fol-lowed. To this question, 30.87 percent (representing 32.1 million people) responded yes. (This group is here called "learners" to distinguish them from the first group of "would-be learners.") Both groups were asked to indicate what reasons for study were very im-portant to them (from items on a list given by the questionnaire); when the responses to these items were added up, the total percent-ages according to the Burgess categories and two more added by the ETS investigators were as shown in Table 14.

These analyses relate to all adult students or would-be stu-dents and do not suggest that one specific motivation leads people to work for the external degree. In the demand study, only 7 per-cent of the learners were seeking academic credit and only 17 per-cent of the would-be learners wanted it. These percentages, how-ever, translate into many millions of people, as shown in Chapter Three.

One additional body of data concerning the motivation of external-degree seekers is available. When the Regents External Degree was announced in New York State, approximately five thou-sand people wrote to express an interest in it. A questionnaire was subsequently sent to these individuals; 1370 people replied. When asked why they were interested in such a degree, slightly more than

[1] P. Burgess, "Reasons for Adult Participation in Group Educational Activities." *Adult Education,* 1971, 22:1, 3–29.

[2] The demand study described in the Preface.

Table 14

REASONS FOR STUDY

	Would-be Learners	Learners
	Percent	
Desire to know	91	87
Desire to reach a personal goal	90	66
Desire to reach a social goal	59	29
Desire to reach a religious goal	31	23
Desire to take part in a social activity	39	27
Desire to escape	30	26
Desire to meet formal requirements	37	31
Desire for personal fulfillment	67	45
Desire for background knowledge	14	8
Other, or no response	18	5

Source: The demand study.

half said that it was for reasons of employment, and slightly less than half answered that it was for self-evaluation or personal satisfaction.[3]

In considering motivation, the nature of a particular external-degree program helps to define the reasons why its students attend. It has been established that the motives which lead adults to learn cannot be inferred from the content they study. Thus an external-degree program in business administration is likely to draw people influenced by all of Burgess' factors (except possibly the desire to reach a religious goal). It is equally true, however, that most will be interested chiefly in reaching a personal goal.

Much more research is needed on the motivation for undertaking the external degree, but discussions among leaders and planners of such programs suggest three general reasons as particularly significant. First, securing a degree is important to the learner for

[3] Data provided by L. B. Koroluk of the Division of Independent Study; State Educational Department; Albany, New York.

economic advantage or maintenance because the knowledge itself is essential.[4] Second, the learner feels a desire for rounded or completed growth which goes beyond the study of specific subject matters to indicate the achievement of some integrated whole of knowledge. Third, society (family, employer, circle of friends) exerts more or less direct pressure on many individuals to achieve the personal status of a college graduate; these pressures may be particularly strong on one who started a program but never completed it.

Will the external degree be regarded as cheap and unworthy? Judged on past American practice, the answer is no. Some of the most outstanding American leaders of government, business, social, and academic life are the products of evening colleges or hold other extension degrees. Once the degree is awarded, it stands as a symbol of accomplishment and is usually accepted as such by an employer, by the individual himself, and by his associates. Other factors intervene, other accomplishments are achieved; and before long the source of the degree is brought to light, if at all, only by the person who received it (or by his biographer) to show his persistence or how far he came in life. The hierarchy of degrees is not as firmly fixed in the United States as it is in other countries, where, for example, a man's obituary may indicate what honors level he reached forty years ago. Here the institution that conferred his degree may sometimes be noted, but that is all.

The reputation of the external degree on the campus itself depends largely on local circumstances. If the degree is reaching a meritocratic elite, has a reputation for excellence, or pays faculty well on an overload basis, it may have high standing with much competition among the academic staff to teach in it. In other cases, it is viewed with reserve, withdrawal, indifference, or scorn; and even the enthusiasts who support it may have dubious motives. In a study of evening colleges reported in 1961, 71 percent of the deans of adult divisions reported that their presidents had a very favorable

[4] In the case of *Griggs* v. *Duke Power Co.*, the Supreme Court ruled 8–0 in 1971 that educational attainments could not be required of job applicants unless the need of such requirements for the specific job in question could be demonstrated to a court's satisfaction. This decision may have a marked influence on the demand for a college degree as a general requirement of employment.

attitude toward their divisions; 23 percent reported a more or less favorable attitude. Further questioning revealed, however, that much of the support of the "very favorable" presidents came from the belief that the divisions could produce income (6 percent), provide a good public-relations image (33 percent), or enlarge the size of the student body by maintaining a program identical to that on campus (27 percent). Only 5 percent of these presidents were thought to have an understanding of the importance of the adult education division as an independent entity.[5]

As with any other part of the institution, the strength and reputation of the external-degree-awarding unit changes over time. This fact may be verified by the histories of such divisions, and a vivid account of how the traditional practices of a university can erode its extension degree is provided by Myrtle S. Jacobson in her study of the pioneering program founded by Brooklyn College.[6]

The value of a particular extension degree has been fairly well established in the minds of those who know it, but the worthiness of adult or assessment degrees remains in question. Little can be said about assessment programs because they are too new to be evaluated, but the record is reasonably good so far as special degrees for adults are concerned. One president reported: "We've had no difficulty. The baccalaureate we offer has been accepted by other institutions and by business and industry, for example, in terms of tuition incentives; all accept it as a basic educational experience." With respect to graduate school admission—potentially the thorniest issue so far as acceptability is concerned—one director observed:

> So far, so good—particularly in terms of graduate admission. About half of our students so far have gone to graduate study, and I think one of the early figures several years back was that eighty-two out of eighty-three applicants for graduate or some form of higher study had been accepted. What we find again and again is that the qualities of autonomy and ability to define and execute independent study

[5] J. T. Carey. *Forms and Forces in University Adult Education* (Chicago: Center for the Study of Liberal Education for Adults, 1971), pp. 98–101.

[6] *Night and Day.*

are precisely those qualities which are treasured in the better institutions of higher learning.

As far as employers go, we have a lot of people in human services, and they tend to be a high autonomy, self-starting group. The constituency which we attract is a very attractive one in terms of initiative. You don't come to our program to accumulate credits and stuff; you really come because you have the potential readiness for some significant change. I think that the kinds of occupation people tend to go into are not security conscious, structured, and corporate, but tend to be more in the education or human services field.

One way of handling acceptance at other institutions is to recognize that "there is a lot of student anxiety about it, especially regarding admission to graduate school and law school." The solution is to "build research about graduate school into someone's learning program, so that it can be developed in terms of those requirements. So if someone's goal includes a particular graduate school, the program is designed with that in mind." As for "employers, personnel groups, and societies," they are "usually pretty supportive, saying that if we can show on-the-job competence, then that's a much better record than someone who's sat for four years in a classroom and requires retraining anyway."

When asked the best way to start an external-degree program in order to insure academic support, the dean of one of the most successful gave the following list of suggestions:

1. In developing and instituting a program, make certain the person who starts writing the formal and informal proposal for the initial program has some status. Make certain that person has a doctorate, is someone on the faculty, is a dean, or a vice-president; someone who cannot be overwhelmed by informal sabotage.

2. Center the development of the program in one of the existing divisions, preferably the strongest, usually the Arts and Sciences College, rather than the extension program.

3. When staff members are being hired, use very high standards. Pick people who are at least as good if not better than people who are being recruited in the other colleges, so that no one can question the credentials of your faculty.

4. The final thing is to be certain that the admissions requirements for students are at least as high as those used in the university in general, at least in the initial few years. That can be deviated from after a while and exceptions can be made, but in the first few years, those students had better come in under the same criteria, or again there's going to be some basis for calling it a second-rate program.

Similar advice is given by the directors of other programs. At one university, for example, the director reported that "the chairman of the curriculum committee was strongly opposed to our program, so we put him on our committee. He was completely converted." And, at still a third institution, "we place emphasis on the amount of interface that goes on between the faculty and the student member. Since, in most cases, the students have considerable background, we try to utilize that in the classroom, to give an even more practical application of the courses."

The question remains as to the attitude of society and the academic community toward the external degrees awarded by new institutions created only to award them and with no record of quality to maintain. Particularly in the conservative academic community, a new institution granting an assessment degree necessarily devalues the customary currency; its degree is not the pure metal of the past but merely a thinly silvered alloy. Unfortunately, this interpretation is correct in some cases; so-called colleges and universities have thrived, though, by any known standards, they were diploma mills. It is equally true that even the most charitably inclined observer must turn away in dismay from some degrees awarded by fully accredited and presumably reputable institutions. The problem lies not with whether a degree is internal or external or whether it is sponsored by an old or a new institution, but with whether it has inherent quality as assessed either formally or informally, a topic considered later in this chapter.

One subject often mentioned in this connection has to do with the relative ability of adults and young people to learn. This issue arises because most external-degree students are grown men and women rather than young people in their immediate postadolescence; some believe that only the latter have the ability to acquire highly organized and systematic knowledge. The results of research show that individuals in external-degree programs are often equal or superior in intellectual capacity to individuals in internal-degree programs. In 1959, Roger DeCrow published a summary of studies comparing adults and young people who take university credit courses. His conclusion was that "there is considerable evidence that adult students are equal or perhaps slightly superior to undergraduate students in learning *performance*. Without exception, in the group tests adults have shown equal or superior learning *ability*."[7] Later studies have led to this same conclusion. Thus, if the external degree is regarded as cheap and unworthy, the fault lies not with the students but with the people who admit, counsel, teach, and evaluate them.

Should nonteaching institutions award the external degree? Almost everywhere in the world, the CNAA being an exception, degrees are awarded only by institutions called colleges and universities, the latter term being by far the more common. But, as noted in Chapter Two, the word *university* can be used as a mask for a government department, as it was for two-thirds of a century by the University of London. The basic issue, however, is not what a degree-awarding institution is called but whether it teaches the students to whom it awards degrees. In the United States, the intimate interrelationship of the two functions has been taken for granted. With some of the new external degrees, the issue of separation is raised; and, if present plans succeed, that separation may well become an enduring part of American education.

Despite wide variation in patterns, both here and abroad, the external degree is given on one of three bases: (1) The certifying institution evaluates the accomplishments of the student and takes no responsibility for his instruction; (2) The certifying insti-

[7] R. DeCrow, *Ability and Achievement of Evening College and Extension Students* (Chicago: Center for the Study of Liberal Education for Adults, 1959), p. 10.

tution approves the work of non-degree-granting institutions and awards the degree on the basis of the completion of that work, sometimes also setting further requirements before doing so; (3) The certifying institution provides its own instruction and also undertakes evaluation. The University of London External Degree Program typifies the first form, the CNAA the second, and Birkbeck College the third. In the United States, the New York Regents Degree is most like the first approach, the second has no parallel (though the Commission on Accreditation of Service Experiences described in Chapter Three suggests credit equivalencies but grants neither credits nor degrees), and the third is a common occurrence.

The chief target of traditionalists' dislike (as it has been for a century and a half) is the first of these patterns. Can an institution conscientiously award a valued degree on the basis of examinations passed by people its staff may never have seen? To anybody aware only of the long and honorable tradition of American higher education, the only answer is no. However, perhaps the sharpest attack ever launched against the practice was made by a group of British leaders who ended a lengthy essay on the subject with the following peroration:

> *Examinations, even when conducted by the teachers of the university and based upon the instruction given by them, ought not to be the only tests for the degree. It is not right that the work of years should be judged by the answers given to examination papers in a few hours. It cannot be fairly tested in this way. However conducted, such examinations are an insufficient and inconclusive test of the attainment of a university education; and when account is taken of individual idiosyncracies and the special qualities which examinations favor, and when allowances are made for the accidents which inevitably attend such limited and occasional tests, it appears to us only fair that due weight should be given to the whole record of the students' work in the university. If the academic freedom of the professors and the students is to be maintained—if scope for individual initiative is to be allowed to the professors, and the subjects are to profit to the full by their instruction—it is absolutely*

*necessary that, subject to proper safeguards, the degrees of
the university should practically be the certificates given by
the professors themselves, and that the students should have
entire confidence that they may trust their academic fate
to honest work under their instruction and direction. There
is no difficulty whatever in the university providing for such
control, regulation, and publicity as will be an adequate
guarantee of impartiality and of such a measure of unifor-
mity as may be considered desirable.*[8]

This comment, made in 1913 by a Royal Commission, was,
as noted earlier, sharply repudiated some years later by the committee appointed to carry out its recommendations. At that subsequent date, the University of London itself requested that the external-degree system be kept in force. And, while a degree awarded
on this basis has been constantly attacked ever since, any such attack brings into question all of British higher education. While internal degrees require much more than the passing of a culminating
examination, the honors level of the degree is based quite firmly
upon it, and its construction and grading are determined by examiners who may never have taught the students whose papers they
read.

Part of the problem with the external degree in Britain is
the fact that so many different degrees, from the humblest to the
most exalted, are offered. Nothing of this sort is seriously proposed
in the United States yet. Instead, those who argue for an external
degree of any sort usually believe that the A.A., the baccalaureate,
or the master's degree should come first and that each or all should
be offered in a limited range of subject matters, usually in general
or liberal studies or in business administration. If these first ventures
succeed, an expanded program can be developed later. Meanwhile,
let everyone be cautious!

Viewed with caution and against the long, rich history of
the University of London, it seems reasonable to offer to Americans
a degree wholly by examination. To be sure, the ultimate test lies
in the capacity of the examination itself to evaluate such programs,

[8] *Final Report,* p. 36.

but as expertise grows and the range of available measuring instruments—practical as well as theoretical—becomes broader, there seems no valid reason why a person wishing a degree should not be able to test his or her capacity solely by examination. Because of the profusion of other opportunities available, particularly if the recommendations of the Commission on Non-Traditional Study are adopted, few people may avail themselves of this option; but arguments against trying it—and then, when sufficient data exist, evaluating the results—deny opportunity to people who might otherwise secure a degree.

How essential is residence or collegial experience in a degree program? The previous question dealt with the value of direct contact between instructor and student; we now turn to the educative effect on students of association with other like-minded but diverse people. Many regard the question of residency as the chief difference between an internal and an external degree. But what is residence? Traditionally the student leaves his home and goes to live in a university community, often in facilities provided by it or at least in a situation where its presence is deeply felt. Many believe that a community of professors and students working together and in association makes up an essential part of a college or university degree. (This is best exemplified, perhaps, by the German seminar or the Oxford or Cambridge college.)

Some people agree with John Henry Cardinal Newman that it is the crucial element. If he had to choose, he said in 1852, "between a so-called university, which dispensed with residence and tutorial superintendence and gave its degrees to any person who passed an examination in a wide range of subjects" and "a university which had no professors or examinations at all, but merely brought a number of young men together for three or four years," he would not hesitate to say that the second would provide "the better discipline of the intellect."[9] This famous passage has resounded through the years, reinforcing the tradition of the university as a community of scholars and saying that it also ought to be a community of students—in fact, that the latter was essential to higher education. The

[9] J. H. Cardinal Newman, *The Idea of a University* (New York, Longmans, Green, 1910), p. 145.

Royal Commission of 1913, citing Newman as its authority, lists as the first essential of a university education the fact that "the regular students of the University should be able to work in intimate and constant association with their fellow students, not only of the same but of different Faculties, and also in close contact with their teachers."[10] This idea continues to be powerful; as noted in Chapter Five, much modern research on college and university life has to do with how student culture based on residence establishes and perpetuates itself.

If Newman is correct, then the external degree is a mockery and only a "so-called university" would provide it. This issue arose at the University of London in 1856 when it was first proposed to permit students who had not studied at an affiliated college to present themselves for the external degree. An immediate outcry was heard from the alumni, the majority of whom were against the idea; since they had secured their degrees by attendance at classes, so should everybody else. But a minority view prevailed, using an argument which read in part: "The assumption that without college training there can be no effectual guarantee that a candidate is sufficiently respectable, i.e. of sufficiently high social position, is too manifestly illiberal to need refutation. This is narrowing the question of a candidate's fitness to a test of his parents' pecuniary resources. It would not be wise to assume that a young man has studied seriously and conducted himself with propriety because his friends have maintained him for two years at a college. But the young man who presents himself for examination in the confidence of knowledge acquired by dint of self-denial and self-reliance, brings the strongest presumptive evidence of intellectual and moral culture."[11]

As higher education has grown in size and greatly broadened it constituency, the residence argument has become less important.

[10] Newman, p. 26.

[11] Quoted in: P. Dunsheath and M. Miller, *Convocation in the Universtiy of London* (London: Athlone Press, 1958), pp. 148–150. If the original author of the quotation had read the next section of Newman's book, as perhaps he did, he would have found the Cardinal (somewhat inconsistently) agreeing with him, though holding that "few indeed there are who can dispense with the stimulus and support of instructors."

Certainly those who try to make the absence of collegiality the barrier to the external degree fight an uphill battle at present. A very
large number of American students working toward internal degrees
have very little contact with faculty members or other students except in class. Like the students at Scottish or continental European
universities, they live where they wish or must, ride the bus or subway to campus for their classes, do their required reading in the
library, and use student amenities sparingly if at all. And the term
residence credit has been so distended that it is now used by many
institutions for work done at distant extension centers, some of them
outside the United States.

On the other hand, planners of external degrees have gone
to great lengths to establish some vestiges of collegiality. The London External Degree Office and the Open University both offer
short residential courses for their students. Many of the adult and
assessment degrees now in effect in the United States or planned
for the near future make use of periodical conferences or short
courses lasting from one to four weeks and providing highly intensive and usually residential interaction among teachers and students.
For example, the Goddard College program requires its students to
meet for two weeks every six months, and its directors argue the
great importance of such study: "Because its matrix is the human
world in which individuals are gregarious and symbiotic, [adult degree program] study begins and ends in the social microcosm of the
two-week resident period. During this residence students are challenged and assisted, shaken loose of some preconceptions, introduced to some brand-new notions, and given every opportunity to
learn from and with each other, from and with concerned and intelligent teachers. Often a student begins the resident period with a
firm notion of what he wants to study during the coming six months
and leaves it with a detailed plan for studying something completely
different—the end product of hours of conversations with persons
whose experiences are totally different from his own and who see
the world in another light than he does. Residential adult education succeeds because it fosters the sharing of experience."[12]

Similar accounts exist of the intensity of the residential seg-

[12] Pamphlet issued by Goddard College.

ments of other external-degree programs, though many are more highly structured than the ones at Goddard. In fact, it is ironic but true that an external-degree program may occasionally provide more true collegiate association than do the courses of study of many programs awarding internal degrees.

A deeper issue is also worth noting. In the American tradition of the college, residence under supervision was necessary in part because of the youth of the students. Piety and discipline underlaid scholarship, but not so deeply that they were invisible. Educators believed that young men and women should be brought out of the sheltered world of their homes and their earlier schooling gradually and guided to a large and complex world view and to the capacity to move easily and effectively in this world. The change from boyhood to manhood or girlhood to womanhood could best be carried out by acculturation—older and more knowledgeable members serving as models and mentors for younger and more innocent ones. The belief in collegiality is also based on sustained interaction among youths—causing them to enlarge the understanding and change the behavior of one another. To carry collegiality over to programs for people long past adolescence may be to confuse means with ends.

Will the external degree so depersonalize the educational process that the needs and desires of individual students will be lost? Some danger of depersonalization exists with external-degree programs, particularly if students are removed geographically from access to mentors and counselors. At the present time, virtually all directors of new programs are carefully handpicking their students, offering them elaborate counseling and guidance, providing introductory services to help them achieve or regain learning skills and reestablish confidence in their educational abilities, and setting up banks of data concerning backgrounds and accomplishments. As one director observed, "This kind of program requires an enormous amount of intensive counseling" and then immediately added, "It would be easy to let that slip." Bailey has pointed out rightly that learning, by whatever method, is often difficult; and it may prove to be unusually so in external-degree programs. "Enormous expectations will be initially established followed by the thud of mass attrition. For years, many correspondence schools have come close

to fraud by making exorbitant profits from the actuarially determined drop-outs of their sullen systems of lonely learning."[13]

The only real safeguards against the loss of personalization
lie in designing and financing programs which allow for a great deal
of contact between teacher or counselor and student and which
make use of vigilant administrative pressure to be certain that student learning needs are met. The belief that, eventually, teaching
can be turned over to the machine is doomed to failure, though
such has been a fond hope of some since audiovisual education became prominent in the 1920s. Sometimes systems can be established
in which a machine alerts a mentor, a counselor, or an administrator that a student is in trouble, but ultimately humans must be
helped by other humans. This may dash the hopes of those who believe that by the use of the mass media and electronic devices the
cost of the external degree can be less per student than that of the
internal degree.

*How can students with varied academic accomplishments
fit them together into a meaningful degree pattern?* As Chapter
Three shows, many Americans have acquired college credits by
various routes: attendance at one or several colleges, passing CLEP
or other examinations, CASE equivalency records, and other means.
The academic record of such students is a hodgepodge reflecting
past interests, work assignments, places of residence, ways of life,
and participation in unconventional higher-education institutions.
Many have far more academic credits than they need for a degree
but no way of fitting them into a meaningful pattern. Wide adoption of degree-by-examination can help solve this problem and is
perhaps the best answer since it evaluates current competence, not
that attained some years before.

Another suggestion has been made for dealing with the matter: the creation of a "credit bank" or "educational registry" which
might, for a fee, evaluate transcripts and other records submitted
by the student, see what kind of degree pattern they now make,
and advise him what additional competence he should secure to
round out his record, perhaps referring him to higher-educational
institutions willing to work with him toward completion. It could

[13] Bailey, pp. 4–5.

also keep his "account" open for addition of further credits or equivalencies. A college or university might provide this service, also for
a fee, and award the degree once the student has satisfied the requirements. Or a national, regional, or state consortium of colleges
and universities, perhaps linked with a credit bank, could carry out
the endeavor, each college and university accepting the work done
at the others.

What prohibits full implementation of any such arrangement is that most colleges require that a minimum amount of work
be completed on campus. The supply study found that 71 percent
of American institutions require at least an academic year's work
on their own campus; another 20 percent have lesser requirements.
Data are not available for five percent, and only four percent claim
no residency requirements at all for the baccalaureate. Public institutions are less restrictive in requiring attendance than private institutions.

Residency requirements are usually matters of local academic decision. If a college wished, either independently or as part
of a consortium, to enter into an arrangement in which minimum
attendance was not required of an external student, little other than
making up the deficit in its tuition fees (presumably by some system of equivalency payments) would stop it from doing so. If this
action violated the rules of an accrediting association, leniency probably could be secured for a limited period because of the experimental nature of the program.

*Should external-degree programs be developed in such a
way as to help educate nondegree audiences?* The extension-degree program has almost always served both a degree and a nondegree audience. The evening college, for example, usually opens
its credit courses to qualified nondegree registrants who want to
study the content for its own sake, wish to use the credits for credential purposes, can get reimbursement of tuition from an employer only for a credit course, or think that as long as credit is
available they may as well secure it. In many cases, nondegree students enlarge the audience, making the program possible economically. In other programs, educational activities offered by the mass
media can be heard or viewed by nonregistrants, thereby having
augmented educational effect. Nobody knows how many people

listen to college courses provided by commercial or public television. Presumably the viewing pattern is sporadic, but the presentation of serious and sustained bodies of knowledge to the general public might be a potentially important by-product of the growth of extension-degree programs.

In newer programs, however, serious doubts about considering such secondary audiences are expressed. In most of the adult or assessment degree programs, the sponsors wish to work, at least initially, with a relatively small group of carefully selected people. After the design of the new program is well established, it may be opened up a bit to secondary audiences; but in the early days it may be dangerous to think about them, since the temptation to serve the larger number rather than the smaller is always present.

Many new programs are multimedia in character, requiring the student to read, write, and discuss as well as to watch television and listen to radio. What he watches or hears is therefore intimately related to what he is supposed to learn through the other three methods. If the television producer, for example, thinks too much about his nondegree audience, he may produce a show which does not require other techniques for comprehension, thus minimizing their interactive value. If he permits television to do that best done by other methods, he may neglect the unique contributions his medium should be making.

The issue remains unresolved and is likely to be discussed until a more mature perspective is achieved on the external degree itself and on its place in the whole of adult education.

How can established educational authorities measure the quality of specific external-degree programs? The quality of higher education is presently assured by elaborate systems of accreditation—both of total institutions and of individual programs—and of licensure, in which government exercises its right to examine the practitioners of occupations or to require their certification by recognized private institutions. This complicated network of private and public scrutiny is currently in a state of flux and nobody can predict with assurance its future course. It is too early to say how external degree programs will fare in the long run or to identify those central authorities who will make decisions concerning them.

The immediate reaction to the newer degrees, particularly

by regional accrediting associations, is good. "There's a new openness among them," said one of the most progressive leaders of the external-degree movement, "and we tend to exaggerate the pressures coming from these sources." In another part of the country, the director of a special degree program for adults reports that the administrators of the regional association "told us that we couldn't use them as an excuse for not trying something different"; the director has worked closely with the staff of the association and "appreciated their comments and suggestions." In still a third region, a director reports that the regional association has "been wonderfully cooperative with us in trying to find ways in which we could become part of the mainstream."

Significant formal acceptance of external degrees and other non-traditional programs by a regional accrediting association came in December 1971, when the Southern Association of Colleges and Schools revised its controlling policy to read, "The Commission does not wish to be restrictive on new, special activities of a member institution but rather seeks to encourage innovation and an imaginative approach to providing quality instruction according to the educational needs of the college's constituents." The detailed rules for applying this policy spell out the plans and regulations for non-traditional programs in great detail but with marked openness of viewpoint and an experimental attitude calling for revision at specified future times as more experience is gained.

New institutions solely based on the external degree and not yet accredited feel likely to encounter difficulty in winning immediate acceptance for their programs. One director of a highly experimental program indicated what he felt to be the appropriate strategy in such cases:

> *I think we must challenge the kind of evaluation, whether that be individual evaluation of students by examination or the procedures and criteria of institutional evaluations by accrediting organizations. It is not that they are necessarily wrong but they do need thorough study. And I think the way we should challenge it is not by complaining, or by any kind of accusation, but by the much more difficult and dignified way of saying that here is something un-*

> *like the thing you have been looking at, and we suggest that
> you look at it in ways unlike your present ways. We've not
> begun in this area, though we intend to very shortly. We
> intend to say: Here is what excellence means in our struc-
> ture, and we ask you to consider this kind of excellence.
> Some of the standards will be quite similar, but others will
> be very different. For example, a program advisor who has
> never gone to college is, by conventional standards of excel-
> lence, not excellent; but we ask you to consider his skill to
> do this job quite apart from the fact that he hasn't a col-
> lege degree.*

Everyone who cares about the quality of higher education
must hope that this attitude of reasonableness will be backed up
with solid proof of excellence and that the arbiters of accreditation
and licensure, whether specific or general, private or public, will
demand at least as high standards (though not necessarily the same
standards) of external degrees as they do of internal degrees. Cheap
and easy degrees can already be secured, a fact which is discussed
at every educational conference and erupts periodically in the press.
The external degree must be built not on the denial of the status
quo but on the affirmation of new standards of excellence or new
ways of achieving established standards. As new structures and
processes of accreditation and licensure develop, they must accommodate the new patterns of the external degree, but they must also
guard against uncritical acceptance of all claims made for it.

*Can present teaching methods meet the requirements of the
external degree?* Chapter Three points out that much of the impetus for the external degree arises from the belief that new techniques of teaching and learning have outmoded or will soon out-
mode past techniques. It is interesting, therefore, to see how widely
the new methods have been adopted. A study was made in the summer of 1972 of the teaching methods of 122 non-traditional programs conferring the baccalaureate. The frequency of use of each
method is shown in Table 15.

The methods used in non-traditional programs are still predominantly the conventional ones of the past. Many reasons have
been advanced as to why so little use, even as adjuncts to instruc-

Table 15

TEACHING METHODS USED IN NON-TRADITIONAL PROGRAMS

(N = 122)

Methods	Much Use	Little Use	No Use	No Response
		Percent		
Classroom lecture	40	46	12	2
Tutorial teaching	27	52	20	1
Programmed instruction	5	38	55	2
Computer-assisted instruction	1	18	80	1
Tape cassette instruction	5	36	58	1
Talk-back telephone instruction	...	8	91	1
Closed-circuit, live talk-back television	1	9	89	1
Closed-circuit television or videotape without feedback	2	15	82	1
Broadcast radio or television	1	15	83	1
Field work or cooperative study	35	37	27	1
Correspondence study	12	25	62	1
Short-term campus residency	11	22	67	...
Other	9	4	85	2

Source: Special tabulation provided by Janet Ruyle for the demand study.

tion, has been made of the newer technologies. Among the arguments cited are the cultural lag of educators, the high cost of the new techniques, their relative inflexibility and lack of accessibility, and the fact that they are not efficient on a small scale. Bailey summarizes the core of the problem: "Of course, cassettes and videotapes and cable TV and autotutorial library carrels can help in the instructional process. But in education, hardware is no better than software. If millions of dollars worth of instructional devices are already dustcovered in campus closets, what makes us believe that similar or even more sophisticated devices will save the world off-campus? We are in our infancy in developing academic software suitable to the miracles of instructional hardware. This pattern will not change overnight. A lot of the existing software available for, and advertised as aids to, self-study is unbelievably shoddy."[14]

Meanwhile, the directors of external-degree programs have used ingenuity. As one such person said, "All the ingredients were already there—we simply had never drawn them together in a new pattern." The president of a new college said, "We're encouraging people to reach out to teaching-learning situations all over the metropolitan area—on the job, in their home, in their neighborhoods, while they're playing." A third director emphasizes the need for "an intensive in-service training of faculty in terms of pointing to these new frontiers and different techniques and the respect for autonomy and the individual learner." Special problems are handled in special ways. One university, for example, has developed a special required course for all entrants, a "six-hour course designed to reduce anxiety and rebuild verbal skills, which creates a supportive enclave for the returning adult student."

In Chapter One, the learning options allowed in 112 nontraditional baccalaureate programs are mentioned; the programs show a wide variety of structural ingenuity and diversity. They confirm, however, as do the data in this section, Bailey's observation: "For years ahead, the most valuable learning aid will still be a little pedagogic device called a book." But, as with other cases of cultural lag, the newer technologies of learning will in due time be perfected and utilized increasingly in external-degree programs, either as primary methods or, more probably, as component elements in the broad educational process.

If given a choice, would people select the external or the internal degree? Many people can now choose either an external or an internal degree, and the decision goes both ways. But, for others, the choice is not completely free. Many have one or the other available and must take whichever presents itself. More important, choice is limited for many because the circumstances of their lives—

[14] Bailey.

job, family responsibility, and money—allow only the external degree.

The main thrust of the question, however, lies not with adult students but with the late-adolescents now studying in internal-degree programs. Here, the existence of an option might significantly weaken traditional programs. If many chose the external degree, the number from which colleges and universities select would decrease. More than that, students choosing the internal-degree program might decline so substantially as to create difficulty in its maintainance. The external degree would join the community college as a threat to existing four-year programs.

But the consequences would not necessarily be bad, quantitatively speaking, even for the four-year institutions. Some students who do not want "to go to college" in the usual sense might undertake the less confining experience of the external degree, and a fairly large number might well decide to transfer to a residential setting later on. Students who would otherwise be lost to the system of higher education could be attracted. Moreover, many students enrolled in college drop out for a period of time; as is shown in Chapter Three, a fairly large percentage never comes back. Perhaps these students might be maintained in the system through the unique characteristics of the external degree.

The movement of students can no longer be predicted on traditional assumptions. For example, in a study made in one state, almost as many people transferred into community colleges as transferred out of them; yet the whole discussion of the "transfer" function assumes that the movement is always in one direction. The additional option of the external degree is likely to influence the established patterns of university and college residence in ways which cannot now be predicted.

What will be the ultimate impact of the external degree on institutions of higher learning? The answer can be stated straightforwardly: it will strengthen some of them, perhaps being one means of their survival, and will weaken others, perhaps being one cause of their death. On still a third group, perhaps the majority, it will have no major influence; they have well-defined programs, secure finances, a constant and adequately large flow of applicants, and no desire to do more than fulfill their established missions. As time goes on, they will unobtrusively adopt innovations, some originating in the structures or processes of the external degree.

Less happy will be the institutions weakened by external-degree programs, either their own or those sponsored by other colleges and universities. The age of constant expansion in baccalaureate education has drawn to a close so far as service to young people of customary college age is concerned. (The grandchildren of World War II veterans will provide an increased clientele in the early 1980s; but, for a budgetary officer, the time between now and then seems an eternity.) While the mortality of colleges has been largely absent from the thoughts of American educators for many years, it has come forcefully to attention recently by the death of some institutions, including good ones. Thus a college which commits its resources to an ill-conceived or poorly executed external-degree program may suffer as a result. Alternatively, the existence of a college or university is threatened by a decrease in its scope of service, which can occur when another institution drawing on the same constituency creates an external-degree program. While decline or death may befall an institution because of poor administration or adherence to outmoded policies, difficulty may also arise if a college has too narrow a base of resources to mount successful external-degree programs or is disadvantageously placed geographically to draw student bodies of adequate size. Private institutions are particularly vulnerable because they must charge high fees; they have already been threatened by the increase in the number of low-cost public institutions. The growth of the external degree will not be the sole cause of the decline and downfall of marginal institutions, but it may prove an important contributory factor.

On balance, however, the external degree is likely to have a positive influence on institutions of higher education for three reasons suggested earlier. First, by creating an effective external-degree program, an institution can reach new clienteles not previously enrolled, thus increasing or maintaining its student body and the scope of its service. Second, students in such programs otherwise might never have entered higher education, and the experience of working toward a degree may encourage them to continue their education either at the same institution or another. Third, internal-degree programs may be enriched and given new vitality by the external degree. The latter can introduce new content and methods; if they succeed, they can be used "on campus," thereby continuing the long tradition of innovativeness described in Chapter One. Less tangibly, the teaching of adult students may have a wholesome effect on faculty members who would otherwise have contact with only inexperienced late-adolescents. A forty-year old brings to his study a depth of experience which a twenty-year old cannot match; teaching adults may help shake a faculty member out of orthodox and routine ways.

What are the international implications of the American external degree? Various forms of American adult education—agricultural extension, summer session, and management training—have been widely borrowed and adapted by other countries. But the extension and the adult degree have found few imitators. The master of Birkbeck College in London has spoken with professed envy of "the voracious appetite of North America's working public for higher education," confessing that "my telephone never rings on such matters; in my two years in College I have received no single enquiry from any employer, public or private, concerning the way we might help."[15]

So far as the assessment degree is concerned, the United States is clearly the debtor. Various American plans pay due respects to the University of London and the Open University as creative innovators. But with very few exceptions (such as a comprehensive plan devised but not yet actuated by the Academy for Educational Development), the use of the American degree to serve people of other nations has not been contemplated. This fact contrasts strongly with the English experience: the London external dgree has had profound influence throughout the Empire and the Commonwealth; and the leaders of the Open University are eager to market their materials in other countries.

Some external degree developed in the United States may prove capable either of educating people of other countries directly or of serving as a model for creation of indigenous programs. As yet, however, it is too early to say whether this will happen.

What is the major problem of the external degree? Keeping

[15] Hare.

alive the excitement and interest which it has generated is the greatest problem facing the external degree. The United States has a long record of experimental colleges built on yeasty new ideas. Some maintain a pioneering spirit or rejuvenate themselves with periodic infusions of new ideas, but all too many institutions have fallen prey to routines and to the erosion of time. Mary McCarthy vividly pictures the result in *The Groves of Academe,*[16] and not even Randall Jarrell's counterattack *Pictures From an Institution*[17] takes the curse from what she wrote. One president with unusually good credentials as an external-degree pioneer puts the problem directly: "The way that higher education is structured, what was non-traditional yesterday, if it doesn't become a major commitment of the institution, becomes a rather stale competitor to the traditional departmental offerings. There's a constant gravitation back to the norms which have characterized higher education for the last fifty to a hundred years. So the major problem is how you translate what you've learned through non-traditional studies into living parts of the institution, without getting it structured or isolated."

It would be good to end this chapter by proving that some infallible principle inherent in the external degree will ensure its success. As these two final chapters have indicated, however, many difficult issues remain. Success is not certain, but, as José Ortega y Gasset said in calling for the reconstruction of the Spanish universities, "Man would be badly off, indeed, if he were incapable of enthusiasm except for the things in which he has faith! Humanity would still be pursuing its existence in a hole in the ground; for everything that has made it possible to emerge from the cave and the primeval jungle appeared in its first hour as a highly dubious undertaking."[18]

[16] M. McCarthy, *The Groves of Academe* (New York: Harcourt Brace Jovanovich, 1951).

[17] R. Jarrell, *Pictures From an Institution: A Comedy* (New York: Farrar, Straus, and Giroux, 1954).

[18] J. Ortega y Gasset, *Mission of the University* (Princeton, N.J.: Princeton University Press, 1944), p. 35.

Epilogue

John Summerskill

In the late 1960s, higher educa-
tion in the United States was subject to questioning, restlessness,
and, sometimes, outright rebellion. The mood of confidence preva-
lent among educators since World War II was shaken on the one
hand by students and on the other by those responsible for governing and financing higher education.

During this period, students searching for a different kind
of learning experience beyond secondary school launched various
new endeavors. Experimental or free universities sprang up on a
number of campuses—colleges within colleges where students could
determine the curriculum and the kinds of instructors they wished
to hear from. "Relevance" was the watchword; discussion in the
experimental colleges ranged widely over the ills and aspirations of
mankind, from assassination, death, and poverty to idealistic and
far-reaching plans for a new social order.

Meanwhile, students from previously neglected minorities
were admitted in significant numbers to American colleges and universities. Many of these students used the campus as a base for out-

173

reach work in minority communities. Because they often saw the institutions as predominantly white and racist, they expressed their resentment of the typical college curriculum and the campus climate in which it was embedded. As part of a growing separatist movement, some students demanded and got changes in their instruction as well as a series of new curricula based on ethnic studies, Afro-American studies, and Chicano studies.

By the beginning of the seventies, these and other forces, acting in concert upon institutions, succeeded in opening up the system of higher education. Elements of the curriculum and instructional procedures sacrosanct for decades were suddenly thrown open to question. Experimental programs like ethnic studies and student tutoring in the inner city became woven into the established institutional fabric.

Many faculty listened to the students and agreed with some of their complaints—or at least agreed to investigate them. Alan Pifer, president of the Carnegie Corporation, expressed in his 1971 annual report what many educators were thinking—not only about what was happening but also about what was needed. "The explosive growth of higher education in recent years and the proliferation of functions it performs seem to have destroyed any common sense of purpose within the enterprise. . . . A central task, then, if higher education is to be reformed through reduction of the pressures on it, is the invention of viable alternatives for some young people, alternatives that are at least as productive to society, as useful to the individual, and no more costly than going to college."

It was my fortune at both Cornell University and San Francisco State College to witness, to participate in, and eventually to become a storm center in the revolutionary movements which shook American higher education in the late 1960s. Then, after three years in Ethiopia as an advisor on problems of higher education, I came back to a position which gave me a good vantage point to observe what was happening to American higher education.

In Chapter Four, Houle refers to the joint effort of the College Entrance Examination Board and the Educational Testing Service in providing help and direction to experimental approaches to reconstruct and redirect degree programs throughout the country. As the first director of this effort (now called the Office of New Degree Programs), I had a fine opportunity to examine what was being proposed, how it was being developed, and, more subtly, what was in the minds of educators and citizen policy-makers using the umbrella term *external degree* to describe efforts to fulfill new hopes and aspirations in colleges and universities.

My comments in this Epilogue grow from the observations, reading, and discussion which this position made possible. Conferences, meetings, and reports proliferated; but, more important, it was possible for me in the latter part of 1971 and in early 1972 to visit about thirty-five campuses where non-traditional programs were either underway or under discussion. Looking retrospectively over this period, several things come to mind.

Central Thrusts

There is no overall design to the extensive experimentation marking higher education in the early 1970s. Colleges are going their own ways, experimenting with those aspects of instruction that are either most troublesome or most promising in reform. Throughout the United States, many institutions or systems of higher education have established or are considering the establishment of some type of external-degree program.

But while each is unique, reflecting local institutional arrangements, academic standards, and student concerns, it is possible to differentiate external-degree programs according to four major thrusts—a different curriculum, a new student population, a new kind of faculty, or a novel arrangement of space and time requirements differing vastly from the traditional classroom and schedule. Although one particular thrust may be prominent in the origins of a program, the four are frequently interrelated. By considering each of them separately, we can best describe what is taking place across the country.

Different curriculum. Some external-degree programs recently established in America must be considered primarily in ideological terms. They are experiments in the content of the curriculum—the stuff of learning—and they are distinctly non-traditional. Houle considers a number of these in detail, most notably the large-scale plans of the University of California and of the California State

University and Colleges and the program of the Minnesota Metropolitan State College.

Other colleges and universities have based their external degrees upon the reordering of old bodies of content or the devising of new ones. Such ventures do not demonstrate that American higher education is turning on its heel and marching off to some Valhalla filled with the wisdom of the ages. They simply suggest that some of the impetus behind the new external-degree programs goes well beyond method and technology; the experiments are meant to fulfill revised concepts of what students should learn beyond secondary school.

Concern about students. In various places, external-degree programs have been formulated or planned because of concern about student populations lacking access to post–secondary education. The Open University in Great Britain, promoted from political concern for a working class which had not had wide access to British universities, brings higher education to them in their homes, using especially designed instructional materials and techniques.

The United States has many who have been deprived of higher education, a point documented at length in Chapter Three. Many of the programs described or mentioned in earlier pages originated in the desire to meet the needs of these segments of the population. My own thoughts return to Hawaii and to the special problems and opportunities that the education of its students presents. The chancellor of the University of Hawaii is responsible for all higher education in that state including the community colleges. It is a complex responsibility because the state is composed of seven islands and plenty of Pacific Ocean, and everyone, it seems, wants to go to college. This geographic situation raises a difficult question: does the Chancellor invite everyone to Honolulu and the University of Hawaii or does he try to find ways and means of carrying post–secondary education to the people?

Chancellor Harlan Cleveland and his colleagues have been exploring various arrangements and technologies for externalizing higher education from its Honolulu base to students on all the islands. The extension education system serving people throughout the islands provides a sound base from which to expand. One of the main interests now is in the use of new technologies (television, video cassettes, audio cassettes, and so on) to reach a new and wider extension audience.

Another Hawaiian program of interest was initiated a few years ago at Chaminade College in Honolulu. A private, Catholic, four-year college, Chaminade had a coeducational enrollment of some nine hundred full-time students. In recent years, as costs increased and financial difficulties mounted, the Chaminade administration began to concentrate on a new constituency—the officers and enlisted men on the six major military bases in Hawaii. They found that a substantial number of these servicemen had attended college at various times during their military careers but had had no opportunity to complete requirements for a degree. So Chaminade hired servicemen as counselors, made its course distribution and residency requirements more flexible, and offered its instructional program to military men on their bases at convenient times. In two years the enrollment at Chaminade doubled, and these qualified mature students helped revitalize the college.

New faculty. When colleges offer instruction of a different type to new populations of students away from the lecture hall and laboratory, existing faculty may or may not be interested and supportive. Consequently, institutions with new student clienteles and institutions with new ideas about higher education frequently seek and employ new kinds of teaching faculty to carry out the special processes and procedures in the external degree.

The nomenclature used on many campuses today provides a hint of the kinds of changes that are taking place on the faculty level. At Minnesota Metropolitan State College, for example, the major responsibility for teaching and guidance rests with part-time "practitioners" engaged in the activities of "advising" and "facilitating." At MMSC, advisors negotiate "contracts" with students on an individual basis. One is a long-term contract that may involve several years of study and lead to an undergraduate degree; another is a "project contract" or "subcontract" that covers only the learning program for a few months ahead, including projects on the job, papers to be written under the supervision of professional people in the community, and internship experiences. In addition, the full-time staff advisors identify able "resource people" in the community to guide and instruct students in their various projects.

At Empire State College in New York, one seldom hears the words *faculty, instructor,* or *professor,* but one does encounter a number of *mentors* who work with individual students and negotiate contracts with each for the next steps in their undergraduate education. Unlike Minnesota Metropolitan, Empire States does not offer classroom instruction; the mentors are responsible for referring students to ongoing courses at nearby colleges and universities, helping them develop their own programs and objectives, and informing them about available learning resources.

At the headquarters of the British Open University, the faculty look much like that at any leading British or American university. But at OU, serious faculty discussions center upon such topics as improving the written materials for the foundation course in the humanities or the quality of a recent television tape on quantum theory. The faculty is oriented to the refinement of undergraduate instruction and is recruited from other universities with these objectives always in mind.

In England, as in the United States, the new kinds of faculty may be drawn directly from the community or they may come from institutions of higher learning. At all three of the educational institutions just mentioned, large numbers of queries and applications for faculty positions are received from academically qualified people. Apparently, there are many who would exchange classroom lecturing for the satisfaction of talking with, instructing, and guiding individual students as they move through the educational process.

Time-free, space-free programs. External degrees often originate by establishing instruction at some new time or place more convenient to the student than the customary daytime campus-based classroom. Perhaps the ultimate expression of this idea is the credit-by-examination approach used in the Regents' Degree Program in New York State or at Thomas Edison College in New Jersey. Both programs are reminiscent of the time-honored University of London external-degree program in which it does not matter where the students learn, how they learn, or when they learn, as long as they can demonstrate that, in fact, they have learned.

Many additional experiments are now taking place to provide more flexibility for students in the use of time and space, although some involve a substantial component of residential study. C. W. Post College in New York, for example, has established a weekend college involving two full weekends of formal intensive study and four weeks of independent study, while other programs offer six days of formal classroom study spread over six consecutive weekends. (Post makes its program more attractive with credit-card tuition payments, described by Long Island's *Newsday* under the headline "A Chance to Learn Now, Pay Later.")

An evening and weekend college operating year-round in Denver under the Model Cities Program provides several hundred poverty-area persons with an opportunity to attend college-level classes designed to accommodate their working schedules. This weekend-college project organizes instruction at the request of students and has been able to defray all direct educational costs including tuition, fees, and texts.

Some other universities coordinate their programs with the railroads to accommodate commuting students. Adelphi University on Long Island conducts regular courses on the Long Island Railroad, morning and evening, for students of business administration commuting into and out of Manhattan. Not to be outdone, New York University's School of Continuing Education is now offering two noncredit courses ("Our Changing Economy: Current Trends" and "Literature for the Seventies") aboard New Jersey-to-New York commuter trains. There is some irony in the fact that universities are now imitating the notoriously flexible schedules of New York commuter trains!

Institutions that have long held evening sessions for working students are beginning to think about other kinds of scheduling, including concentrated classroom instruction on a forty-hour-a-week basis. One community college plans to run all its courses in four- to five-week modules to accommodate a student body of working students taking one or two modules a year and regular students taking more. Many junior colleges have been especially attentive to flexible time scheduling such as that pioneered by Mount Vernon College, also in Washington, D.C.

A further variation in the use of space for learning is illustrated by a program in which the Dallas (Texas) Public Library serves as a study center, with the cooperation of faculty from Southern Methodist University and the support of the Council on Library Resources. This program serves students seeking college credit through the College-Level Examination Program. Libraries involved in these programs enter into cooperative arrangements with qualified faculty in various undergraduate fields, and these experts prepare extensive reading guides for students studying on their own. The libraries then acquire and make available necessary books and audiovisual materials, field by field, and provide suitable reading and study space. Information is given about CLEP and other examinations for credit. To meet the fast-growing demand for such examinations, the College Entrance Examination Board has now established some five hundred national examination centers for the CLEP program in locations throughout the United States. It has also established the Office of Library Independent Study and Guidance Projects, a unit designed to encourage and assist libraries in their efforts to support the independent college-level learner.

New Devices and Learning Strategies

To implement most fully the innovative steps previously considered, educators involved with the external degree, like their counterparts in more traditional education, are exploring many new devices and methods.

Printed materials. It is paradoxical that the external degree depends heavily on a tried-and-true method of instruction, the printed page. Home study is hardly new in America; since World War II, however, enrollment in correspondence courses in the United States has grown prodigiously. It is estimated that some three million Americans enroll each year in correspondence courses sponsored by proprietary institutions, the armed services, and universities. Indeed, the United States Armed Forces Institute now annually enrolls 120,000 servicemen worldwide in its correspondence and self-study programs.

The most far-reaching experiment in the development of printed teaching materials is being carried out by the Open University. Instruction in all courses is delivered into the student's home by means of textbooks and weekly lessons prepared especially for independent study. Materials have been developed in five basic foundation courses (arts, mathematics, science, social science, and technology). Specialized work in these courses (and in education)' is in continuing preparation. In each course, after objectives are established, plans are devised to integrate the written materials with periodic television and radio broadcasts. Teams of scholars, educational technologists, and communications experts produce modular lessons that extend, on a weekly basis, through a thirty-six-week academic year. The drafts are reviewed by other scholars and academic officers and are submitted to students for pretest and revision.

Although the development costs for each foundation course are something like $500,000, the results of this investment are worth the cost. The materials are intellectually challenging, well written, presented in logical and provocative sequence, and published with high professional and artistic standards. For assessment and motivation, periodic self-examinations, objective quizzes which students submit for marking by computer, and essay questions which are read by tutors at the end of several lesson modules are provided.

At the University Without Walls, orientation is toward student projects, student participation in community service for learning and credit, and independent study in the home. But the program, which enrolls both residential and part-time students, makes heavy use of books and other printed materials. A recent survey of Harvard seniors shows that books are by far their most preferred mode of learning; thus, it is not surprising that at the University Without Walls, where instruction is highly individualized, there is still great emphasis on book learning among both teachers and students. Perhaps the chief innovator as far as learning materials are concerned was Gutenberg.

Mass media. Experience in America since World War II has dispelled any notion that education has nothing to do with the world of mass media. The fantastic growth of commercial and public television and its impact on opinion, politics, and the economy have been obvious to all. The campus turmoil of the late 1960s provided an unforgettable lesson to faculty members and administrators in the enormous influence of the mass media on their constituents, their governors, and their benefactors.

During the 1960s, closed-circuit television, tape cassettes, and other inventions were used to improve instruction in special circumstances (for example, hospital operating rooms) or to reach special groups of students (postgraduate professionals in teaching, medicine, and other fields). Techniques developed in our society to reach the masses are, however, becoming increasingly more relevant for educational institutions. As students claim the right to higher education, much as previous generations claimed the right to secondary education, universal postsecondary education becomes a probability rather than a possibility. (In California and Utah, the proportion of graduates continuing beyond high school has climbed over 70 percent.)

These experiments have a longer tradition of usage than some educators realize. For fifteen years, the Chicago TV College has provided television instruction for associate degree credit throughout the local viewing area. New York University founded its Sunrise Semester in the fall of 1957 and has subsequently contributed to the degree education of more than eleven thousand students who climb out of bed early each morning to turn on their television sets. But although many other institutions use television tapes to enrich residential and extension education, no detached observer could claim that the medium has profoundly affected either the content or delivery of post–secondary education to date.

The national preoccupation with television does not mean that radio (which is less costly in terms of both production and transmission) will have no role in external-degree education in the future. The Open University has already discovered that radio is effective in transmitting information to students in their homes—a fact well understood by governments and educational and religious institutions in many parts of the world. In Japan, the University of the Air, Asia's first open university, has been launched on a commercial radio network for an experimental period of six months. Four days a week, lessons in domestic science, literature, industrial administration, and engineering are being transmitted to students throughout the country. If the experiment proves successful, a much more ambitious project combining radio and television will be launched.

That most deep-rooted of all mass media, the daily newspaper, may also have a role in transmittting knowledge to students who do not physicially attend college. In 1972 the National Endowment for the Humanities made a grant to the University of California, San Diego for a two-year experiment in which that university and newspapers in selected American cities will cooperate to offer college-level courses to newspaper readers throughout the nation. The pilot course on "America and the Future of Man" and succeeding courses will consist of twenty lectures, each written by a distinguished authority. After a trial run, the lectures will be distributed to participating newspapers across the country. Other universities will be asked to honor credits obtained by examinations following the newspaper series. The newspaper copy will be supplemented by written lecture notes, books or booklets, and self-testing questionnaires.

Audiovisual aids.   In addition to innovation with printed materials for home study and education via the mass media, external-degree programs make use of audiovisual aids such as tapes, photographic slides, and combinations to effect "multimedia" instruction. A professor or academic authority with command of the subject matter must, of course, create the tape or slides, but he does not have to stand in front of his students at all times. In fact, mechanical and electronic devices are increasingly a supplement, or even a substitute, for the classroom and the printed text.

Computer-assisted instruction.   The technological revolution that made television and cassettes available to higher education has also placed another powerful instrument in the hands of educators—the computer.

It has been estimated that by 1975, the amount of computer power devoted solely to education will be equal to the entire computer output for all purposes in 1968. This is not difficult to understand when one considers the enormous usefulness of the computer in individualized instruction. In his paper "Computers in Education," Wayne H. Holtzman of the University of Texas points out: "The keeping track of a person moving at his own pace in a continuous-progress environment where the particular branching of the curriculum is tailor-made for his own learning aptitudes and level requires a computer to manage the curriculum and assist with the instruction. Emphasis is on the learner rather than the teacher. The teacher may be necessary for learning under some circumstances and may actually be a hindrance under others. The student begins at that point in the curriculum where he is best capable of learning and moves at his own rate, with knowledge of his results immediately following his answer. The particular sequence of the curriculum may be controlled almost entirely by a computer or it may be completely under the control of the student, depending on the type of material to be learned, the kind of student, and the purposes of the instruction."[1]

A student using computer-assisted instruction (CAI) techniques as part of an external-degree program typically works in a remote "inquiry terminal" or teaching station where he receives instruction from the computer through the use of recording and playback devices and communicates his responses by typing on a keyboard or actually writing with a pen across the face of a television screen.

Although computer-assisted instruction seems to work best for drilling and practice with highly structured material, some progress has been made in applying CAI to tutorial types of instruction. At the University of Illinois at Urbana, a variety of courses have been devised by the Computer-based Education Research Laboratory. Approximately half of the student's time is spent in the classroom or laboratory, the other half with computers. Donald Bitzer, director of the laboratory, believes that the computer increases the amount of material that can be covered in courses by about 30 percent. Most instructors at Illinois who have used the computer like it because it enables them to concentrate their energies on problem-solving rather than on the rote aspects of teaching.

Cost, of course, is the most important factor blocking the progress of computer-assisted instruction. Professor Bitzer and his colleagues at Illinois have found that, on the average, one hour of computer-assisted instruction requires twenty-six hours of preparation by authors, graphic artists, and others. To be efficient, a university's facility must have a large number of computer terminals available. Professor Bitzer estimates that with four thousand terminals in operation, for example, the cost of instruction can be reduced to approximately thirty-five cents per student-hour.

[1] W. H. Holtzman (Ed.), *Computer-Assisted Instruction, Testing, and Guidance* (New York: Harper and Row, 1971), pp. 1–2.

Although many colleges and universities have computer facilities, most are now used for research rather than instruction.
Moreover, few institutions have any long-range or comprehensive
plans for computer support of instruction. Among the universities
active in CAI are Florida State, Pittsburgh, Pennsylvania State,
Stanford, the State University of New York at Stony Brook, the
University of Illinois, and the University of Texas at Austin.

Multimedia approach. Some universities combine several
of these systems in a multimedia approach to instruction. McGill
University in Montreal is experimenting with modular course units
and multimedia teaching in a variety of disciplines. The administration of this large university is solidly behind innovation, a fact
much appreciated in that academic community. The university has
established a Center for Learning and Development where new
forms of instruction are designed and evaluated. Here, members of
the faculty can transform courses into modular units so that students
can proceed at their own pace. Thus, a student in introductory
psychology, for example, can sign up for eight units in that field and
take the examinations for each unit when he feels he is prepared to
do so. Depending on the courses, students can take advantage of
specially prepared audiotapes, photographic slides, printed materials
designed to assist independent study and supplement traditional
textbooks, or programmed instruction with computer assistance.
Faculty members who have elected to work with the Educational
Research Center to renovate their courses are assisted by a talented
multimedia staff. Freed from too much development work, instructors can spend more of their time in the "Drop-In" center advising
and tutoring individual students enrolled in the modular and multimedia courses.

The Future

The educational experiments described here are, in many
respects, too recent to be placed in firm perspective. Is higher education in America really undergoing a metamorphosis? Are new
and effective ways to educate actually being discovered? Are break-
throughs in the offing with respect to the costs of mass education?
Or is the whole external-degree movement a fad built on the whims

of the disaffected, soon to disappear after irreparably damaging
hard-won academic standards?

There are signs in all sections of the country that the times
demand a new kind of pluralism in postsecondary education. The
large teaching/research university is decreasing in importance as
the prototype for *all* higher education. Universities are becoming
more flexible with regard to admissions requirements, course distribution requirements, and demands for campus residence. To meet
the requirements for many different kinds of sophisticated educational services, state colleges and community colleges have grown
rapidly and have earned for themselves massive financial and political support. Moreover, proprietary schools for vocational and technical education and training programs sponsored by industry and
labor unions currently form the fastest-growing segment of postsecondary education.

This, to the writer, is a movement in the right direction. But
the uncertainty, suspicion, anad resistance which exist in some academic circles should not be underestimated. Proposed changes in
tried-and-true traditions seem to many to threaten academic standards, the allocation and control of academic resources, and even
academic jobs. Consequently, the writer has heard much from faculty members and others who are unconvinced that there is anything of substance to non-traditional education. To some, the very
ideas of the external degree, credit by examination, and independent study deny those basic values and practices upon which their
whole profession is founded.

Regardless, colleges are changing and will continue to change
because the society which supports, uses, and ultimately controls the
educational system is changing. It will be best if the academic community itself gets to work on the issues and takes full leadership in
planning and implementing the kinds of educational innovation required by diverse categories of postsecondary students.

Bibliographic Essay

Cyril O. Houle

In dealing with the literature related to the external degree, the reader soon discovers himself confronting a sea of material largely made up of announcements, brochures, prospectuses, news accounts, pamphlets, theses and dissertations, inexpensively duplicated reports, and lists of requirements and regulations. Stringent limitations have therefore had to be placed on the scope of this bibliography. Items designed to be permanent have been chosen over those intended to be temporary. Background materials are mentioned only briefly, largely to indicate that they exist. Less attention is paid to the extension than to the adult and assessment forms of the external degree since readers are likely to be more interested in the new than in the familiar. Peripheral materials—such as essays on cable television, video cassettes, or the theory of testing—have been largely excluded, even though they might mention external degrees. Finally, primary (though far from exclusive) attention is devoted to American institutions and practices, since the worldwide literature is largely unavailable to American readers.

187

The reports, journals, and records of proceedings of three national associations are particularly rich with materials on various aspects of the external degree. They are the Association of University Evening Colleges (AUEC), the National University Extension Association (NUEA), and the Center for the Study of Liberal Education for Adults (CSLEA). Although the third of these is deceased, during its lifetime it issued a particularly significant series of monographs dealing with the adult degree. While several of its publications will be listed later, its whole series of monographs and occasional papers is worth examining by the serious student of the subject, as are the publications of the two national associations. The CSLEA series has been carried on and expanded by Syracuse University in its various publications dealing with adult education.

News coverage of the external degree—especially the assessment degree—has been widespread in the daily and weekly press and in journals of opinion. The *Chronicle of Higher Education,* in particular, has carried many news stories and feature articles on the subject.

Adult Education

Traditionally, most students in extension degree programs, both here and abroad, have been adults, though that fact may be much less true in the future than in the past. A few particularly relevant references from this field will therefore be suggested as background for the subsequent more detailed items.

No adequate history of adult education has been written, but the best single volume is C. Hartley Grattan's *In Quest of Knowledge: A Historical Perspective* (Association Press, New York, 1955). This discursive essay on the growth of adult education through the ages has an excellent account of the transfer of the English extension service to the United States. In *A History of Adult Education in Great Britain from the Middle Ages to the Twentieth Century* (Liverpool University Press, Liverpool, 1970), Thomas Kelly provides an excellent general background to the history of all adult education in Great Britain with particular reference to the growth of university efforts. The best American history, which includes university extension as one aspect of the whole field, has been provided by Malcolm S. Knowles in *The Adult Education Movement in the United States* (Holt, Rinehart, and Winston, New York, 1962). A number of special institutional histories also exist. Two excellent examples are *The Boundaries of the Campus: A History of the University of Wisconsin Extension Division, 1885–1945* (University of Wisconsin Press, Madison, 1957), by Frederick M. Rosentreter, and *A History of Adult Education at Columbia University* (Columbia University Press, New York, 1954), by John Angus Burrell.

The *Handbook of Adult Education* (Macmillan, New York, 1970), edited by Robert M. Smith, George F. Aker, and J. R. Kidd, but written by many authors, is probably the best single source of information concerning the alternate systems of education with which universities and colleges must work or compete. The results of a national sampling study on the students in adult education are provided in *Volunteers for Learning* (Aldine, Chicago, 1965) by John W. C. Johnstone and Ramon J. Rivera. A. A. Liveright and David L. Mosconi report a status survey of the extent of continuing education in the United States which emphasizes the work of colleges and universities (and which, by a process of peer review, identifies the institutions now regarded as "the pace-setters" and "the comers") in *Continuing Education in the United States: A New Survey* (Academy for Educational Development for the National Institutes of Health, New York, 1971).

A number of volumes have focused on higher adult education. Probably the best of these is *University Extension* (Center for Applied Research in Education, New York, 1965), in which Theodore J. Shannon and Clarence A. Schoenfeld provide a broadly descriptive account of general practice. An annual summary of enrollments in extension classes, correspondence courses, and conferences is published jointly by the AUEC and the NUEA under the title *Programs and Registrations. The New York Times Guide to Continuing Education in America* (Quadrangle Books, New York, 1972), edited by Frances Coombs Thomson, is a general directory of opportunities for continuing education in the United States, giving central attention to the offerings of institutions of higher learning.

Two recent issues of international journals are devoted to the role of universities in adult education in various countries, with emphasis on innovative practices: volume 4(3) (1971) of *Convergence*, and a much fuller worldwide survey in the *Journal of the International Congress of University Adult Education, 11* (May 1972).

Renee Petersen and William Petersen are sharply critical of higher adult education in *University Adult Education: A Guide to Policy* (Harpers, New York, 1960). An early effort to identify major directions and a call for complete redesigning of degree programs for adults was made by Cyril O. Houle in *Major Trends in Higher Adult Education* (CSLEA, Chicago, 1959). The most modern account of the needs of higher adult education, however, is presented in two publications of the American Council on Education. One is Malcolm S. Knowles' *Higher Adult Education in the United States: The Current Picture, Trends, and Issues* (ACE, Washington, 1969). The other, a policy statement identifying and explaining the implications of twelve major propositions, is *Higher Education and the Adult Student* (ACE, Washington, 1972).

General Higher Education

The volume of printed material concerning higher education issued each year is enormous, including as its central core about six hundred books and reports. Clearly, then, the entries chosen for this section of the bibliography are illustrative, not complete. Only items that bear directly on the external degree itself are mentioned.

A first consideration is the nature of the academic degree itself; the most widely read and available historical and analytical account of that subject is presented by Walter Crosby Eells in *Degrees in Higher Education* (Center for Applied Research in Education, New York, 1963). Stephen H. Spurr attempts both to analyze present degree structures and rationalize a plan for awarding them in *Academic Degree Structures: Innovative Practices* (McGraw-Hill, New York, 1970). G. Lester Anderson reacts to this plan in "Academic Degree Structures—A Point of View," *College Management, 7* (Spring 1972).

The perennial feeling that higher education needs general reform has been particularly intense since about 1965, and attacks on the system have often identified problems which could be solved, at least in part, by establishing the external degree, though the critics themselves were not always aware of that fact. Some of the more or less reasonable viewers-with-alarm have been

HAZEN FOUNDATION, *The Student in Higher Education* (Hazen Foundation, New Haven, Conn., 1968)

CLARK KERR, "New Challenges to the College and University" in KERMIT GORDON, editor, *Agenda for the Nation* (Brookings Institution, Washington, 1968)

FRANK NEWMAN and others, *Report on Higher Education* (U.S. Government Printing Office, Washington, 1971)

CARNEGIE COMMISSION ON HIGHER EDUCATION, *Reform on Campus: Changing Students, Changing Academic Programs* (McGraw-Hill, New York, 1972)

The problem of determining who should have access to higher education, in what kinds of institutions, and for what reasons has been widely studied and discussed. The basic issues have been dealt with from many points of view in the following references.

ERIC ASHBY, *Any Person, Any Study* (McGraw-Hill, New York, 1971)

W. TODD FURNISS, editor. *Higher Education for Everybody?* (American Council on Education, Washington, 1971)

ORGANISATION FOR ECONOMIC CO-OPERATION AND DEVELOPMENT. *Equal Educational Opportunity* (OECD, Paris, undated)

Various efforts have been made to examine the patterns of college and university attendance and completion, both in the past and in the projected future. Three such studies are

JOHN K. FOLGER, HELEN S. ASTIN, and ALAN E. BAYER, *Human Resources and Higher Education* (Russell Sage Foundation, New York, 1970)

STEPHEN B. WITHEY and others, *A Degree and What Else?* (McGraw-Hill, New York, 1971)

PAUL TAUBMAN and TERENCE WALES, *Mental Ability and Higher Educational Attainment in the 20th Century*

(National Bureau of Economic Research, Washington, 1972)

The need to plan for the new kinds of students now entering colleges and universities has been dealt with in two books by K. Patricia Cross: *Beyond the Open Door* (Jossey-Bass, San Francisco, 1971) and *New Students and New Needs in Higher Education* (Center for Research and Development in Higher Education, University of California, Berkeley, 1972). A comprehensive study of the American community college with particular reference to its egalitarian functions is provided in *Breaking the Access Barrier* (McGraw-Hill, New York, 1971), by Leland L. Medsker and Dale Tillery. The motivations of the students themselves are examined by Michael Marien in "Beyond Credentialism: The Future of Social Selection," *Social Policy, 2* (September–October 1971), and in a refined statistical fashion by Paul Burgess, "Reasons for Adult Participation in Group Educational Activities," *Adult Education, 22* (January 1971).

Many former college drop-outs would presumably find the external degree suitable for their needs. Eric Ashby, in the book already cited, identifies the drop-out as being a much more common phenomenon in the United States than in England. John Summerskill demonstrates that students, for various reasons, have dropped out of college at a fairly constant rate since the nineteen-twenties in "Dropouts from College" in Nevitt Sanford, editor, *The American College* (Wiley, New York, 1962). The most sophisticated study of such drop-outs, which takes into account the phenomenon of transfer from one college to another, is Alexander W. Astin's *College Dropouts: A National Profile* (American Council on Education, New York, 1972).

A number of writers have examined change in institutions of higher learning, and among the general works on this subject are

EDUCATIONAL POLICY RESEARCH CENTER, *Alternative Futures and Educational Policy* (Stanford Research Institute, Menlo Park, California, 1970)

JAMES HARVEY, *Reforming the Undergraduate Curriculum:*

Problems and Proposals (ERIC Clearinghouse on Higher Education, Washington, 1971)

HAROLD L. HODGKINSON, *Institutions in Transition: A Study of Changes in Higher Education* (McGraw-Hill, New York, 1971)

STEPHEN H. SPURR, "Changing Patterns in Graduate Education," *Journal of Higher Education, 42* (October 1971)

JOHN COYNE and TOM HERBERT, *A Guide to Alternatives to Traditional College Education in the United States, Europe, and the Third World* (Dutton, New York, 1972)

Several major proposals for achieving profound change in higher education have been made, but space permits mention of only a few. In the long run the most significant such work (which deals with all education, not merely higher education) is *Learning to Be* (UNESCO, Paris, 1972), in which Edgar Faure and others project a design of worldwide learning for the balance of this century. The committee headed by Frank Newman is to make a second report presenting its solutions to the problems identified in its first report. The actual document is not available at this writing, but draft chapters have been widely circulated and Newman has given "A Preview of the Second Newman Report" in *Change, 4* (May 1972). Among other works making serious proposals for change are

B. LAMAR JOHNSON, *Islands of Innovation Expanding: Changes in the Community College* (Glencoe Press, Glencoe, Illinois, 1969)

SAMUEL B. GOULD, *Today's Academic Condition* (McGraw-Hill, New York, 1970)

ASSEMBLY ON UNIVERSITY GOALS AND GOVERNANCE, *A First Report* (American Academy of Arts and Sciences, Boston, 1971)

CARNEGIE COMMISSION ON HIGHER EDUCATION, *New Students and New Places: Policies for the Future Growth and Development of American Higher Education* (McGraw-Hill, New York, 1971)

CARNEGIE COMMISSION ON HIGHER EDUCATION, *Less Time, More Options* (McGraw-Hill, New York, 1971)

G. KERRY SMITH, editor, *New Teaching, New Learning* (Jossey-Bass, San Francisco, 1971)

GEORGE B. STROTHER, "Report of the View-of-the-Future Committee," *NUEA Spectator, 36* (June 1972)

The Commission on Non-Traditional Study has issued four publications, of which the present volume is one, dealing with its recommendations for the future of higher education. The major report is *Diversity by Design* (Jossey-Bass, San Francisco, 1973), and an earlier pamphlet published by the Commission itself in 1971 was called *New Dimensions for the Learner*. The other volume already issued is *Explorations in Non-Traditional Study* (Jossey-Bass, San Francisco, 1972), edited by Samuel B. Gould and K. Patricia Cross. Additional research reports of the Commission's work are forthcoming.

Substantial proposals or actions having to do with the reconstruction of higher education are common throughout the world. Three volumes which deal with this topic on a multinational basis are

BARBARA B. BURN, *Higher Education in Nine Countries* (McGraw-Hill, New York, 1971)

STEPHEN D. KERTESZ, editor, *The Task of Universities in a Changing World* (University of Notre Dame Press, Notre Dame, Indiana, 1971)

HERBERT E. STRINER, *Continuing Education as a National Capital Investment* (W. E. Upjohn Institute for Employment Research, Washington, 1972)

The active rebuilding of higher education in Great Britain in the past ten years has profound implications for the external degree. The report entitled *Higher Education* prepared by the Great Britain Committee on Higher Education (Her Majesty's Stationery Office, London, 1963) has led to many changes. It is ordinarily referred to as the Robbins Report after its chairman, Lord Robbins, and its initial effect was assessed by Richard Layard, John King, and Claus Moser in *The Impact of Robbins* (Penguin Books, Harmondsworth, Middlesex, 1969). An unusually brief and brilliant summary of British higher education is presented each year by W. H. G. Armytage in an article entitled "The Universities of Britain" in the *Commonwealth Universities Yearbook,* published annually by the Association of Commonwealth Universities, London. (This entire volume is a valuable source of information concerning the work done by the Commonwealth universities.) A recent effort to survey the broad terrain of British higher education is *Patterns and Policies in Higher Education* by George Brosan and others (Penguin Books, Harmondsworth, Middlesex, 1971).

Extension Degree

The general literature of adult higher education reviewed earlier contains many references to the extension degree. This section will deal more specifically with the provisions of the degree itself or with the institution which typically administers it, the evening college.

That institution has been analyzed and described in relatively comprehensive fashion by a number of authors. John Dyer's book *Ivory Towers in the Market Place: The Evening College in American Education* (Bobbs-Merrill, Indianapolis, 1956), though now somewhat old, remains the standard work on the evening college as the second-chance institution for people who are essentially white-collar workers; it is unusually well-written and has many vignettes which describe practices used and individuals served. Ernest E. McMahon, in *The Emerging Evening College* (Teachers College, Columbia University, New York, 1960), makes a strong case that the college and the degree should be autonomous and not subject to the generalized controls affecting the resident degree. James T. Carey, in *The Development of the University Evening College as Observed in Ten Urban Universities* (CSLEA, Chicago, 1961), compares practices in various institutions. The desirable future for the institution and the degree is presented by Cyril O. Houle in "The Evening College," *Journal of Higher Education, 25* (October 1954) and by five other authors in *A Live Option: The Future of the Evening College,* edited by Kenneth Haygood (CSLEA, Boston, 1965).

Administrative and instructional practices of various institutions have been studied systematically by a number of authors. James T. Carey's examination is entitled *Forms and Forces in University Adult Education* (CSLEA, Chicago, 1961). In recent years, the Research Committee of the AUEC has undertaken biennial assessments of institutional practices. The most recent of these, edited by William A. Hoppe, is *Policies and Practices in Evening Colleges, 1971* (Scarecrow Press, Metuchen, N.J., 1972), which is particularly interesting because it is remarkably similar to another study issued two years earlier and having the same editor, author, and publisher.

Several researchers have studied extension degree students, but most of their reports are still unpublished and are not readily accessible. However, three analyses of particular interest here are available. James T. Carey's study *Why Students Drop Out: A Study of Evening College Student Motivations* (CSLEA, Chicago, 1953) has much to say to those who sponsor external degrees. Roger De Crow, in *Ability and Achievement of Evening College and Extension Students: A Report* (CSLEA, Chicago, 1959), reviews existing studies on the relative ability and achievement of internal and extension students and concludes that the latter are usually at least as able as the former. Christopher Duke describes "Part-Time Students in England" in the *Journal of the International Congress of University Adult Education, 7* (April 1968).

Extension degrees in professional fields tend to be offered by the professional school itself rather than being administered by the university's general evening school. In some cases, as in law, the degree may be conferred by an institution especially created for that purpose. This latter fact has given rise to substantial controversy. Charles D. Kelso's book *The AALS Study of Part-Time Legal Education: Final Report* (Association of American Law Schools, Washington, 1972) makes a long and statistical analysis of part-time legal education, and the author's summation suggests a great deal: "To those who would like to see evening education terminated, this study must surely be disappointing. The Study Director makes no such recommendation. Others may find in the data the basis for a different view. However, the Study Director sees no reason for the AALS to change its present policy of extending membership to schools which have evening programs." A bibliography of the literature on this subject is presented on pages 36–38 of *Legal Education: A Selective Bibliography* (Oceana Publications, Dobbs Ferry, New York, 1970), compiled by Dusan J. Djonovich.

Two major studies of higher education for business, both made in 1959, dealt fully with the extension degree as well as the adult degree, which had already emerged at a number of institutions. They are

> ROBERT A. GORDON and JAMES EDWIN HOWELL, *Higher Education for Business* (Columbia University Press, New York, 1959)
>
> FRANK C. PIERSON and others, *The Education of American Businessmen* (McGraw-Hill, New York, 1959)

Adult Degree

There are few separate treatments of any substantial sort on the adult degree alone, since accounts or analyses of it have so often been mixed with accounts of the assessment degree. Therefore this section will be relatively brief because many of the items in the next section are concerned—often indistinguishably—with both of these external degree forms.

Of the general references, perhaps the most thoughtful is *The University Education of Mature Students,* containing four addresses given at a conference on this subject at Birkbeck College, The University of London, July 20–22, 1967 (published by the College, 1967). This conference was also summarized in a paper by A. L. Mackay, "The University Education of Mature Students," *Universities Quarterly, 22* (March 1968). The first systematic and full-scale study of the adult degree in the United States, with descriptions of programs at seven institutions, is given in *New Directions in Degree Programs Especially for Adults* (CSLEA, Chicago, 1963) by A. A. Liveright and Roger De Crow. The *Proceedings of a National Conference on Special Adult Degree Programs* (Center for Continuing Education, University of South Florida, Tampa, 1970) summarizes a meeting of about eighty experts on the adult degree who spent several days discussing various theories and issues. Roy Troutt, in *Special Degree Programs for Adults: Exploring Non-*

traditional Degree Programs in Higher Education (American College Testing Program, Iowa City, Iowa, 1971), concentrates on the University of Oklahoma program but also refers to developments at other institutions as well as to the whole movement toward external degrees.

A powerful statement of the need for treating adults differently from young people, both instructionally and administratively, is provided by John S. Diekhoff in *The Domain of the Faculty in our Expanding Colleges* (Harper, New York, 1956). A detailed, well-written, and theoretically based analysis of the problems encountered in developing a pioneering adult degree, even in an institution which is relatively sympathetic to it, is provided in *Night and Day: The Interaction Between an Academic Institution and Its Evening College* (Scarecrow Press, Metuchen, N.J., 1970), by Myrtle S. Jacobson.

Except as already noted, descriptive accounts of adult degree programs are not yet abundant in the literature. J. L. Traver analyzes several such programs in *A Study of Adult Degree Programs in Selected American Colleges and Universities* (University of Utah, Salt Lake City, 1969). J. E. Burkett and Paul G. Ruggiers in *Bachelor of Liberal Studies: Development of a Curriculum at the University of Oklahoma* (CSLEA, Boston, 1965) describe the early days at their own institution. Kevin Emmett Kearney's chapter on "The Bachelor of Independent Studies—Adult Degree Program" in *Improving Education for Older Adults*, edited by Andrew Hendrickson and George F. Aker (Florida State University, Tallahassee, 1972), describes the program at the University of South Florida in Tampa.

Assessment Degree

As already noted, judgment must be exercised in allocating references to the three categories of external degree, particularly since the distinction among the three is being advanced—and rather tentatively, at that!—for the first time in this book. Many of the following titles use other terms and their usage will be followed, but in the judgment of the author, they all fall within the category here being dealt with.

The external degree is usually said to have begun with the foundation of the University of London. Eric Ashby in *Universities: British, Indian, African* (Harvard University Press, Cambridge, Mass., 1966) gives a brilliant historical account of higher education in these three parts of the world, with a full treatment of the growth and spread of the external degree. In the early part of the twentieth century, two British governmental bodies probed deeply into the London external degree. The first report was strongly negative; the second, and prevailing, report was highly positive.

ROYAL COMMISSION ON UNIVERSITY EDUCATION IN LONDON, *Final Report* (His Majesty's Stationery Office, London, 1913)

GREAT BRITAIN BOARD OF EDUCATION, *Report of the Departmental Committee on the University of London* (His Majesty's Stationery Office, London, 1926)

Two general histories of the University of London also pay substantial attention to the external degree. Douglas Logan's is entitled *The University of London* (Athlone Press, London, 1962); the other is *Convocation in the University of London* by Perry Dunsheath and Margaret Miller (Athlone Press, London, 1958). Many other works, both American and foreign, also deal with the external degree in some fashion but no general history of it could be found.

In the past several years, many symposia have focused solely on the assessment degree or included it as one of several subjects to be discussed.

Toward the Open University: External Degree Opportunities (Division of Continuing Education, State University of New York at Buffalo, 1971)

CHARLES DAVIS, editor, *The 1,000 Mile Campus* (Office of the Chancellor, California State University and Colleges, Los Angeles, 1972)

"Nontraditional Learning," *Science Education News,* April 1972.

DYCKMAN W. VERMILYE, editor, *The Expanded Campus* (Jossey-Bass, San Francisco, 1972)

Generalized proposals for an assessment degree had been

made in the 1960s and even earlier, but full-scale endorsements of
the idea were not advanced in a fully developed fashion until 1970.
By far the most influential paper on the subject was Alan Pifer's
address "Is It Time for an External Degree?" *College Board Review, 78* (Winter 1970–1971). The full potential of such a degree
was explored by Jack N. Arbolino and John R. Valley in "Education: The Institution or the Individual," *Continuing Education,
3* (1970). Two much fuller documents on the same theme were
written by the same authors but are available (if at all) only in
multilithed form. One is *A Plan for the Study of the Promise and
the Problems of an External Degree* and the other is *The Need, the
Issues and the Strategy: A Companion Paper to a Plan for the
Study of the Promise and the Problems of an External Degree,* both
issued by the Educational Testing Service, Princeton, N.J., in 1970.

A selected list of other generalized proposals follows.

BERNHARDT LIEBERMAN and DEBORAH WYCOFF, *National Bac-
calaureate Examinations: A Proposal for a Drastic
Change in the Conduct of Undergraduate Education*
(University of Pittsburgh, Pittsburgh, 1970)

ROBERT J. SOLOMAN, "Giving Credit Where It's Due," *Educational Record, 51* (Summer 1970)

DAVID E. APTER, "And Now, the University College," *College
Board Review, 82* (Winter 1971–1972)

STEPHEN K. BAILEY, "Education and the Pursuit of Happi-
ness," *UCLA Educator, 14* (Fall 1971)

HENRY A. BERN, "Universities Without Campuses," *Educational Leadership, 28* (January 1971)

ERNEST L. BOYER and GEORGE C. KELLER, "The Big Move to
Non-Campus Colleges," *Saturday Review, 54* (July
17, 1971)

BERNADETTE DORAN, "The External Degree Program; Credits
Without Classes," *College and University Business, 51*
(October 1971)

WILLIAM J. DRISCOLL, "A Rationale for Independent Study
Degree Programs," *School and Society, 99* (November
1971)

W. TODD FURNISS, *External Degrees: An Initial Report*
(American Council on Education, Washington, 1971)

W. TODD FURNISS, *Degrees for Nontraditional Students* (American Council on Education, Washington, 1971)

EWALD B. NYQUIST, *The External Degree: Challenge and Opportunity* (AUEC, Norman, Okla., 1971)

"Students Enroll in Without Walls University," *College Management, 6* (October 1971)

CAROL HERRNSTADT SHULMAN, "A Look at External Degree Structures," *College and University Bulletin, 25* (November 1972)

The very idea of the assessment degree has provoked much uneasiness among American educators, some fearing that it might be a fad and others arguing that it would result in a cheap degree. Such points of view have been expressed in a number of the references already cited even though their tone was generally positive. On the other hand, R. H. Reid's *American Degree Mills: A Study of Their Operations and of Existing and Potential Ways to Control Them* (American Council on Education, Washington, 1959) seems particularly relevant today.

Other references which suggest some of the difficulties and limitations of the assessment degree are

A. VITTULI and others, "How Long Is a Credit, When Is a Course?" *College and University, 45* (Summer 1970)

AARON FEINSOT and EFREM SIGEL, *Breaking the Institutional Mold* (Knowledge Industries Publications, White Plains, N.Y., 1971)

FRED A. NELSON, "The External Degree," *National ACAC Journal, 16* (September 1971)

MICHAEL MARIEN, "Higher Learning in the Ignorant Society," *The Futurist, 6* (April 1972)

FLOYD B. FISCHER, "Uneasiness in an Era of Romance," *The NUEA Spectator, 36* (June 1972)

LEONARD FREEDMAN, "Degree Programs for Adults: Fad or Commitment," *The NUEA Spectator, 36* (September 1972)

The most widely used references describing the assessment degree, even though issued only in multilith form (and, to some extent, the two earlier forms of external degrees), have been inventories of activities and proposals compiled periodically by John R. Valley, recently issued in printed form as *Increasing the Options* (Educational Testing Service, Princeton, N.J., 1972). Since most of the assessment degrees are still fairly young, their progress reports have been issued, if at all, in unprinted form, though several are included in the symposia publications already cited in this section. A few other available reports are

> C. G. ERICKSON, H. M. CHAUSOW, and J. J. ZIGERELL, *Eight Years of TV College: A Fourth Report* (Chicago City College, Chicago, 1964)
>
> L. RICHARD OLIKER, "An External Degree in Business Administration," *Collegiate News and Views, 25* (Spring 1972)
>
> UNION FOR EXPERIMENTING COLLEGES AND UNIVERSITIES, *Universities Without Walls: A First Report* (Antioch College, Yellow Springs, Ohio, 1972)
>
> HERBERT LONDON, "University Without Walls: Reform or Rip-Off?" *Saturday Review, 55* (September 16, 1972)

Despite widespread skepticism that Britain's Open University will ever be transplanted intact to the United States, its basic conception and certain of its methods have aroused great interest in this country with the result that many accounts of its nature and features have appeared. The following very brief list draws from a vast number of articles describing OU as it has appeared to various observers during the short period of its existence.

> NELL EURICH and BARRY SCHWENKMEYER, *Great Britain's Open University: First Chance, Second Chance, or Last Chance?* (Academy for Educational Development, New York, 1971)
>
> W. TODD FURNISS, *England's Open University: A Model for America?* (American Council on Education, Washington, 1971)
>
> STUART MACLURE, "England's Open University," *Change, 3* (March–April 1971)
>
> JOHN WALSH, "The Open University: Breakthrough for Britain?" *Science, 174* (November 12, 1971)

GERALD H. READ, "The Open University in Britain," *Phi Delta Kappan, 53* (December 1971)

JOHN ROBINSON, "The Open University as a Co-operative Enterprise," *Adult Education* [British], *44* (January 1972)

PETER J. SMITH, "Britain's Open University: Everyman's Classroom," *Saturday Review, 55* (April 29, 1972)

One of the most significant events in bringing the assessment degree to the attention of the American public was its central place in the inaugural address of Ewald Nyquist, *The Idea of the University of the State of New York* (State Education Department, Albany, N.Y., 1970). In assuming the twin posts of Chancellor of the University and Commissioner of Education, he made clear that he intended to press hard for the establishment of the external degree and has since done so. Many officials, boards, and commissions in other states have explored the significance of some form of external degree for their own states or constituencies. Of the many available, four such reports are

Report of the Committee on New Institutions to the Board of Higher Education (Illinois Board of Higher Education, Springfield, Ill., 1971)

UNIVERSITY OF CALIFORNIA, PRESIDENT'S TASK FORCE ON THE EXTENDED UNIVERSITY, *Degree Programs for the Part-Time Student: A Proposal* (Berkeley, 1971)

CONNECTICUT COMMISSION FOR HIGHER EDUCATION, *External Degrees and College Credit by Examination: Interim Report* (Hartford, Conn., 1972)

FRED J. HARCLEROAD and ROBERT J. ARMSTRONG, *New Dimensions of Continuing Studies Programs in the Massachusetts State College System* (American College Testing Program, Iowa City, Iowa, 1972)

Facilitative Plans and Mechanisms

As noted in the text of this book, a number of plans and inventions facilitate a climate in which the external—and particularly the assessment—degree can develop. Only a few of them are considered here, chiefly because extending the coverage would gradually lead to a list of unmanageable proportions.

Certainly one important feature of the current scene is the development of tests of college-level achievement. This idea arose somewhat independently in a number of places at about the same time. *College Without Classes: Credit Through Examinations in University Adult Education* (CSLEA, Boston, 1961) was an early survey to ascertain what was being done about giving credit or advanced standing by examinations at that time. The first broad statement about the College Level Examination Program (CLEP) was made by Jack N. Arbolino in *The Council on College-Level Examinations* (College Entrance Examination Board, New York, 1965). A long series of publications, reports, and pamphlets has emerged as this program developed. A similar series has eventuated from the College Proficiency Examination Program (CPEP), which is constructed and administered by the State Education Department in New York.

Various research studies have examined these programs. For example, Margaret C. Fagin reports that "CLEP Credit Encourages Adults to Seek Degrees," in *College Board Review, 81* (Fall 1971). Amiel T. Sharon in *The Non-High-School-Graduate Adult in College and His Success as Predicted by the Tests of General Educational Development* (Educational Testing Service, Princeton, N.J., 1972) reports on the comparative performance in college of those who complete high school by the usual means and those who secure an equivalency certificate by passing a GED test. Sharon has also compared the CLEP scores of college sophomores and servicemen who had not studied beyond the high school level, as reported in "Adult Academic Achievement in Relation to Formal Education and Age," *Adult Education, 21(4),* 1971.

Assessing adult experience in terms of college grades remains a difficult task, one which is discussed in many of the general references already cited. A report on the experience of Brooklyn College in this respect was presented by Bernard H. Stern in *Never Too Late for College* (CSLEA, Chicago, 1963). The work of evaluating armed services courses is reported in many places but perhaps most comprehensively in *A Guide to the Evaluation of Educational Ex-*

periences in the Armed Forces (American Council on Education, Washington, 1968), edited by Cornelius P. Turner.

Perhaps the major work dealing with independent study is Allen Tough's book *The Adult's Learning Projects* (Ontario Institute for Studies in Education, Fall 1971). Robert Dubin and T. C. Traveggia in *The Teaching-Learning Paradox: A Comparative Analysis of College Teaching Materials* (Center for the Study of Educational Administration, University of Oregon, Eugene, 1968) demonstrate by a review of the research literature that a student learns as well through independent study as he does through classroom instruction.

Alternate systems of education (outside the usual school-college-university framework) are analyzed in the *Handbook of Adult Education,* referred to earlier. An effort to canvass the numbers of people engaged in such systems was made by Stanley Moses in *The Learning Force* (Syracuse University Publications in Continuing Education, Syracuse, N.Y., 1971), and Robert J. Blakely and Ivan M. Lappin have explored *New Institutional Arrangements and Organizational Patterns for Continuing Education* (Syracuse University Press, Syracuse, 1969). Amiel T. Sharon reviews the literature on how alternate forms of study could be used for academic credit in *College Credit for Off-Campus Study* (ERIC Clearinghouse on Higher Education, Washington, 1971). David L. Reich describes how "A Public Library Becomes a CLEP Learning Center" in *College Board Review, 81* (Fall 1971).

The use of new forms of technology for educational purposes has attracted the attention of many people and is particularly significant for anyone interested in the external (and especially the assessment) degree. Some of the more important and recent works on the subject are

"Toward the Global Village," *Saturday Review, 53* (October 24, 1970)

ROBERT J. BLAKELY, *The People's Instrument: A Philosophy of Programming for Public Television* (Public Affairs Press, Washington, 1971)

SLOAN COMMISSION ON CABLE COMMUNICATIONS, *On the Ca-*

ble: The Television of Abundance (McGraw-Hill, New York, 1971)

CARNEGIE COMMISSION ON HIGHER EDUCATION, *The Fourth Revolution: Instructional Technology in Higher Education* (McGraw-Hill, New York, 1972)

CARNEGIE COMMISSION ON HIGHER EDUCATION, *The More Effective Use of Resources: An Imperative for Higher Education* (McGraw-Hill, New York, 1972)

CATHERINE R. DOBSON and DONALD G. LEATHERMAN, "Educational Technology: A Selected Bibliography," *Educational Technology, 12* (May 1972)

The Field of Educational Technology: A Statement of Definition (Association for Educational Communications and Technology, New York, 1972)

ROGER E. LEVIEN, *The Emerging Technology: Instructional Uses of the Computer in Higher Education* (McGraw-Hill, New York, 1972)

The problem of financing the external degree has not been dealt with in any comprehensive fashion, particularly in relation to the assessment degree. Three studies which have some bearing on the matter may, however, be mentioned. Richard I. Ferrin in *A Decade of Change in Free-Access Higher Education* (College Entrance Examination Board, New York, 1971) examines the growth of education which was provided at little or no direct cost to the student during the years from 1958 to 1968. An extended analysis of the combined work-study plan of education is provided by Asa A. Knowles and associates in *Handbook of Comparative Education* (Jossey-Bass, San Francisco, 1971). The argument that new methods of instruction can be effectively and economically used only if their special benefits are taken into account is presented by Lawrence P. Grayson in "Costs, Benefits, Effectiveness: Challenge to Educational Technology," *Science, 175* (March 17, 1972).

Bibliographies

Most of the references already cited have lists of readings and a few are themselves bibliographies on special topics. The following items, however, deal broadly with the external degree or with the whole field of nontraditional study.

> *Evening College Education: Basic Information Sources* (ERIC Clearinghouse on Adult Education, Syracuse, 1967)
>
> R. L. FLAUGHER, M. H. MAHONEY, and R. B. MESSING, *Credit by Examination for College-Level Studies: An Annotated Bibliography* (College Entrance Examination Board, New York, 1967)
>
> H. A. BERN, *Universities Without Campuses: Bibliography of Educational Leadership* (Association for Supervision and Curriculum Development, Washington, 1971)
>
> *Bibliography on Aspects of Non-Traditional Study in Higher Education* (ERIC Clearinghouse on Higher Education, George Washington University, Washington, 1971)
>
> HANNAH KREPLIN, *Credit by Examination: A Review and Analysis of the Literature* (Ford Foundation Program for Research in University Administration, Berkeley, 1971)
>
> MICHAEL D. MARIEN, *Essential Reading for the Future of Education: A Selected and Critically Annotated Bibliography* (Syracuse University Research Corporation, Syracuse, N.Y., 1971)
>
> ANN Z. SMITH, "Non-Traditional Study," *Education Recaps* (Educational Testing Service, Princeton, N.J., 1971–1972). This publication, issued ten times a year, annotates current developments in the field of higher education. Several issues were devoted to nontraditional study and the external degree and many other issues devote some attention to these matters.
>
> MARJORIE AMOS FLETCHER, *The Open University, the External Degree and Non-Traditional Study: A Selected Annotated Bibliography* (American College of Life Underwriters, Washington, 1972)
>
> CYRIL O. HOULE, "Bibliographic Essay," *The Design of Education* (Jossey-Bass, San Francisco, 1972). This bibliography deals with the whole process of program-build-

ing in adult education, not merely with that designed to award degrees.

MICHAEL D. MARIEN, *Alternative Futures for Learning: An Annotated Bibliography of Trends, Forecasts, and Proposals* (Syracuse University Research Corporation, Syracuse, undated)

ROLLAND G. PAULSTON, *Non-Formal Education* (Praeger, New York, 1972)

HUGH A. STEVENSON and WILLIAM B. HAMILTON, editors, *Canadian Education and the Future: A Select Annotated Bibliography, 1967–1971* (University of Western Ontario, London, Ontario, 1972)

BETSY S. WALKUP, *External Study for Post-Secondary Students* (CEEB and ETS Office of New Degree Programs, New York, 1972). A supplement to this list was issued later the same year.

Index

A

Ability level and expansion of education, 80–84.

Accreditation and non-traditional programs, 164–166

Administrative-facilitation model, 93

Administrators, and external degree programs, 138–140

Admissions: to graduate school, relation of external degree to, 152–153; open, 65–66, 85, 96–97. *See also* individual colleges and universities

Adult degree: 9–12, 89–90; bibliography on, 197–198; definition of, 15; and innovations, 12–13; institutional problems for, 130–131; *modes-of-learning* model and, 93; Oklahoma University program and, 11–12

Adult education: bibliography on, 188–190; growth in, 66–67; and Open University, 34–38

American Council on Education, 57, 70

Apartheid, 40–41

ARBOLINO, J. N., 10, 75, 91–92

ARLT, G. O., 6–7

Armed Forces, Industrial College of the, 70–71, 204–205

ARMYTAGE, W. H. G., 19

ASHBY, E., 20, 38, 62, 63, 83–84

Assessment and evaluation: acceptance of by business, 152–153; of accomplishment, 69–76; descriptive bibliography on, 203–206; at CCV, 107; and degree requirement flexibility, 10–11; and external/internal degree equivalences, 23–24; general problems in, 127–129; of high school equivalency, 56–59, 65–66; of life experience, 71–73; of military experience, 70–71; at MMSC, 103–104; modifications of since World War II, 69–76; of non-traditional programs, 164–166; and Regents external degree, 94–97; of RLS, 117–118; of UWW, 113–116; by written examination, 73–74

Assessment degree: 90–91; bibliography on, 198–203; definition of, 15; formulation and influence of, 119; institutional problems for, 130–131

Association of University Evening Colleges (AUEC), 89–90, 188

ASTIN, A. W., 52, 53, 84

ASTIN, H. S., 81